Banking's Path To Tech Evolution

Banking's Path To Tech Evolution

Rafeal Mechlore

Grace Publishers

CONTENTS

INDEX

INTRODUCTION

In a period characterized by determined mechanical development and quick computerized change, the financial business has arisen as a key member in the worldwide monetary scene. Banking, a deep rooted establishment, has generally been related with traditionalism, custom, and steadiness. Notwithstanding, throughout recent many years, banking has gone through a significant change that is reshaping how monetary administrations are offered, got to, and made due. This change, frequently alluded to as "banking's way to tech development," addresses a urgent change in the business' elements and practices, driven by headways in data innovation, changing shopper inclinations, and a moving administrative scene.

The tale of banking's tech development is one of ceaseless variation, driven by a basic to stay pertinent and serious in this present reality where the speed of mechanical change is consistently speeding up. It is an account of how conventional physical banks are being reshaped into educated, client driven monetary organizations, and how fintech new companies and computerized financial stages are rocking the boat. This development envelops a great many mechanical developments, including the ascent of internet banking, the reception of portable applications, the rise of blockchain and cryptographic money, the development of man-made reasoning, and the rising spotlight on network safety.

In this exhaustive investigation of banking's way to tech advancement, we will dive profound into the starting points of this change, its key drivers, and the complex manners by which it is reshaping the business. From the earliest digitization endeavors to the present status of open banking and decentralized finance, this excursion through time and innovation will reveal insight into the powers pushing banking into another period. We will likewise analyze the possible advantages and difficulties related with this development, and what it is meaning for different ners, including banks, controllers, clients, and society at large.

The Advanced Day break of Banking

The narrative of banking's tech development starts with the coming of computerized innovation, which ignited a major change in the business' tasks and client communications. This will take a verifiable viewpoint, following the beginning of computerized banking and the most vital moves towards online monetary administrations.

We will investigate the advancement of the web, the introduction of web based banking, and the expansion of ATMs as antecedents to the computerized unrest in banking.

The Ascent of Portable Banking

As cell phones became omnipresent, another in financial's tech development unfurled. In this , we will analyze how portable banking applications have reclassified client accommodation and admittance to monetary administrations. The rise of cell phones and the improvement of versatile banking applications changed the manner in which clients deal with their records, make exchanges, and access monetary data. We will likewise investigate the difficulties of portable banking, for example, security concerns and the significance of client experience.

The Fintech Upset

Fintech, short for monetary innovation, has been a main impetus behind financial's tech development. This will dive into the ascent of fintech new companies and their effect on the monetary administrations industry. We will investigate the different fragments of fintech, from installments and loaning to robo-counselors and insurtech. Fintech's capacity to advance rapidly, offer client driven arrangements, and challenge conventional financial models has reshaped the serious scene.

Blockchain and Digital money

Blockchain innovation and cryptographic forms of money like Bitcoin have presented another layer of development and intricacy to banking. This will examine the capability of blockchain in smoothing out monetary exchanges, lessening extortion, and further developing straightforwardness. It will likewise address the ascent of cryptographic forms of money, their reception by customary banks, and the administrative difficulties presented by these computerized resources.

Computerized reasoning in Banking

Man-made consciousness (artificial intelligence) is changing the way in which banks work, from client support chatbots to gamble with the board and misrepresentation recognition. In this , we will investigate the combination of artificial intelligence in banking, its advantages in customizing client encounters and streamlining functional proficiency, and the moral and security concerns encompassing computer based intelligence in the monetary area.

Open Banking and Information Sharing

Open financial drives are driving more prominent straightforwardness and rivalry in the monetary business.

This will look at the idea of open banking, the sharing of client information between monetary foundations, and how it engages purchasers with additional decisions and customized administrations. We will likewise address the difficulties of information security and protection in an open financial biological system.

Online protection and Administrative Difficulties

With expanded digitalization comes a more noteworthy requirement for online protection and hearty administrative systems. This will investigate the advancing scene of network safety in banking, including the rising danger of cyberattacks and the endeavors to safeguard delicate monetary information. It will likewise talk about the job of controllers in guaranteeing the security and sufficiency of the monetary framework.

Monetary Incorporation and Tech Development

The tech advancement in banking can possibly resolve issues of monetary consideration by growing admittance to monetary administrations. In this , we will talk about how advanced banking and fintech can overcome any issues for the unbanked and underbanked populaces, offering them new open doors and admittance to the worldwide monetary framework.

The Eventual fate of Banking

In the last we will look into the precious stone ball to imagine what the eventual fate of banking could resemble as innovation keeps on progressing. We will investigate ideas like decentralized finance (DeFi), quantum registering, and the job of huge tech organizations in reshaping the financial scene. The will likewise talk about the expected difficulties and moral contemplations in this consistently developing scene.

1. The Changing Landscape of Banking

The financial business, when portrayed by impressive physical organizations and moderate practices, is going through a seismic change. This development, energized by innovative progressions, moving purchaser ways of behaving, and administrative changes, is reshaping the actual quintessence of banking. The scene of banking is going through a significant transformation, with conventional financial models being tested, and new, imaginative players arising. In this investigation, we will unwind the changing scene of banking, analyzing its drivers, challenges, and the extensive ramifications it conveys.

1. **Mechanical Development: An Impetus for Change**

   The coming of computerized innovation has been an essential impetus for the change of the financial scene. Conventional banks, long-laid out as actual organizations with in-person collaborations, have been constrained to adjust to the advanced period. The ascent of web based banking, versatile applications, and advanced installment stages has generally modified the manner in which clients associate with their banks. Clients can now play out many monetary exchanges from the solace of their homes or while in a hurry, in a general sense changing the client bank relationship.

Portable banking, specifically, has turned into a foundation of this change. The universality of cell phones has permitted clients to get to their records, move assets, and make installments effortlessly. This shift has provoked customary banks to put vigorously in computerized foundation and give consistent on the web and versatile financial encounters, guaranteeing they stay serious in an undeniably advanced world.

2. **The Fintech Upheaval: Upsetting Conventional Banking**

   One of the most unmistakable disturbances to the conventional financial scene has come as fintech organizations. Fintech, a combination of "monetary" and "innovation," addresses a different gathering of tech new businesses that offer monetary administrations through creative computerized arrangements. These deft, client driven organizations have represented a huge test to laid out banks, offering imaginative options in contrast to conventional monetary items and administrations.

   From shared loaning and advanced wallets to robo-consultants and digital currency trades, fintech organizations are altering the manner in which people access and deal with their funds. They offer quicker, more helpful, and frequently less expensive arrangements, undermining the piece of the pie of customary banks. This opposition has constrained customary banks to reconsider their contributions, smooth out their tasks, and become more client centered to stay significant.

3. **Administrative Changes: A Moving Scene**

   Banking has forever been a vigorously controlled industry, and administrative changes play had a significant impact in the developing financial scene. In the result of the 2008 monetary emergency, legislatures overall carried out a progression of changes intended to guarantee the soundness and respectability of the monetary area. These changes, going from stricter capital prerequisites to expanded straightforwardness and consistence measures, have fundamentally influenced how banks work.

   One critical model is the development of open financial guidelines in numerous nations. Open financial commands that banks share client information with approved outsiders, encouraging rivalry and development in the business. While this sets out new open doors for fintech firms and different players, it likewise presents critical difficulties regarding information protection and security.

4. **Client Driven Banking**

   The changing financial scene is intrinsically client driven. Banks are progressively zeroing in on understanding and meeting the advancing necessities of their clients. This shift towards client driven banking is energized by the ascent of advanced banking and the accessibility of immense measures of client information.

Present day buyers expect customized and advantageous financial encounters. They need to get to their records, make installments, and get monetary guidance from their cell phones with negligible problem. Banks have answered by putting resources into easy to understand portable applications, chatbots, and simulated intelligence driven answers for upgrade client connections and offer custom-made types of assistance. The point is to assemble further client connections, encourage trust, and advance client unwaveringness.

5. **Branchless Banking and Cost Decrease**

   The changing scene of banking has likewise prompted a reexamination of the conventional bank office. With the ascent of computerized banking, numerous clients are presently directing their monetary undertakings while never going to an actual branch. Therefore, banks have been reevaluating their physical presence and looking for ways of decreasing working expenses.

   Branch terminations and scaling down have become normal systems to cut costs, diverting assets towards computerized advancements and client support upgrades. While this change might bring about cost reserve funds for banks, it likewise raises worries about the possible effect on networks, admittance to monetary administrations, and the fate of the actual bank office.

6. **Information and Examination: Upgrading Independent direction**

   Information has turned into a basic resource in the cutting edge financial scene. The tremendous volume of information created by clients' exchanges, communications, and online ways of behaving furnishes keeps money with the chance to acquire bits of knowledge into client inclinations, evaluate risk all the more precisely, and distinguish false exercises.

   This has prompted the expanded utilization of information examination, AI, and man-made brainpower in banking.

   Information investigation permits banks to settle on additional educated choices, foster prescient models for credit scoring, and customize monetary items and showcasing. Notwithstanding, it likewise raises worries about information protection and security, particularly during a time of expanded digital dangers.

7. **Network protection: A Developing Objective**

   As banks progress to advanced stages and tackle the force of information, they become ideal objectives for cyberattacks. The developing financial scene has presented a more elevated level of online protection risk. The expanded dependence on computerized channels, open banking, and information sharing presents new weaknesses that vindictive entertainers can take advantage of.

   Banks are putting vigorously in network safety measures to safeguard client information, impede digital dangers, and guarantee the uprightness of their advanced stages. This continuous fight among network safety and digital dangers is a characterizing component of the cutting edge financial scene.

8. **Monetary Consideration and Availability**
   One certain result of the changing financial scene is an expanded spotlight on monetary incorporation. As advanced banking and fintech administrations grow, they can possibly carry banking and monetary administrations to underserved populaces. Versatile banking and advanced wallets can give admittance to essential monetary administrations for people in areas with restricted admittance to conventional financial framework.
   This accentuation on monetary consideration lines up with worldwide advancement objectives and endeavors to diminish financial variations. It shows the way that innovation can be tackled to make positive social effect.
9. **The Fate of Banking: Developing with Vulnerability**

The advancement of the financial scene is nowhere near total, and what's in store is overflowing with vulnerability. Arising advancements, for example, blockchain, quantum registering, and decentralized finance (DeFi), can possibly additionally upset the business. The job of huge tech organizations in finance is likewise a subject of discussion, as they have the assets and mechanical ability to reshape the financial scene.

The speed of progress in the financial business proceeds to speed up, and customary banks should stay coordinated and versatile to flourish in this quickly advancing scene.

B. Importance of Tech Evolution in Banking

The financial business, long known for its moderate practices and a conventional way to deal with business, is presently going through a wonderful change, generally determined by innovative headways. The tech development in banking isn't simply a pattern; a central shift has previously modified the manner in which monetary establishments work and collaborate with clients. In this 900-word investigation, we will dive into the significant significance of tech development in banking, featuring how it upgrades effectiveness, openness, security, and client experience while additionally driving advancement and guaranteeing the business' proceeded with pertinence.

1. **Improved Productivity and Cost Decrease**
   Innovation in financial assumes a urgent part in upgrading functional effectiveness and cost decrease. With the appearance of advanced banking and robotization, numerous normal financial cycles have become quicker and more smoothed out. This has permitted banks to fundamentally lessen difficult work and functional expenses.
   For instance, the robotization of record the board and exchange handling diminishes the requirement for human mediation, reducing down on managerial expenses. Furthermore, computerized stages work with paperless exchanges, decreasing administrative work and related costs. These efficiencies empower banks to dispense assets all the more decisively, put resources into creative administrations, and give savvy answers for clients.

2. **Availability and Comfort**
   Tech development in banking has introduced another period of availability and accommodation for clients. The ascent of internet banking, versatile applications, and computerized installment stages implies that financial administrations are not generally limited by actual branches or explicit active times. Clients can now get to their records and play out a large number of exchanges from anyplace, whenever.
   Portable banking, specifically, plays had a huge impact in upgrading openness. With most of the worldwide populace possessing cell phones, banking administrations are at the fingertips of almost everybody. The accommodation of versatile banking applications for really taking a look at balances, moving assets, and making installments has upset how clients connect with their banks. This upgraded openness benefits people as well as independent companies that can deal with their funds in a hurry, consequently expanding their efficiency.
3. **Security and Extortion Counteraction**
   During a time where digital dangers are a steady concern, the tech development in banking is similarly urgent for security and misrepresentation counteraction. Banks have put vigorously in cutting edge network safety measures to safeguard their frameworks and, all the more significantly, the delicate monetary information of their clients.
   Encryption, biometric validation, and multifaceted confirmation have become standard security highlights in present day financial frameworks. These advances cooperate to guarantee that client information stays secure, forestalling unapproved access and possible extortion. Also, AI and computerized reasoning are utilized to distinguish peculiarities in exchanges and expeditiously recognize and forestall false exercises.
   With regards to online installments and advanced wallets, security highlights, for example, tokenization and continuous exchange observing further reinforce client trust. With these high level safety efforts set up, tech advancement in banking improves proficiency as well as shields the monetary prosperity of clients and the honesty of the monetary framework.
4. **Client Experience and Personalization**
   One of the main benefits of tech advancement in banking is the emphasis on further developing the client experience. Present day purchasers expect customized and advantageous financial administrations, and innovation engages banks to follow through on these assumptions.
   Client information, gathered through different advanced channels, empowers banks to make customized encounters. For instance, information examination and man-made reasoning assist keeps money with figuring out client inclinations, permitting them to offer custom-made monetary items and administrations. Chatbots and remote helpers upgrade client collaborations, offering

continuous help and addressing requests every minute of every day.

Besides, portable applications and online stages are planned with easy to understand interfaces, guaranteeing clients can explore their monetary undertakings effortlessly. The comfort of computerized banking has turned into a significant selling point for banks, drawing in clients who esteem consistent and customized encounters.

5. **Development and Rivalry**

   Tech development in banking has prodded a flood of development and expanded rivalry. The ascent of fintech (monetary innovation) organizations, with their light-footed way to deal with making computerized monetary arrangements, has provoked conventional banks to advance and stay cutthroat.

   Fintech new businesses offer imaginative options in contrast to conventional monetary items and administrations, going from distributed loaning and robo-guides to cryptographic money trades and computerized wallets. These developments have expanded the scope of choices accessible to purchasers, making a more unique and cutthroat scene.

   Accordingly, conventional banks have embraced a more pioneering mentality, cultivating inward development labs and investigating organizations with fintech firms. This cooperative methodology brings permitted banks to the table for imaginative arrangements that stay up with client requests, while likewise utilizing their laid out standing, administrative experience, and broad client base.

6. **Administrative Consistence and Detailing**

   Tech advancement in banking has extraordinarily worked on the business' capacity to consent to an undeniably complicated administrative climate. Guidelines administering banking activities have become more rigid in the outcome of the 2008 monetary emergency. With trend setting innovation, banks can smooth out consistence methods, create extensive reports, and guarantee exact information assortment.

   Computerized detailing instruments assist keeps money with submitting administrative reports precisely and on time, diminishing the gamble of resistance and related punishments. This shields the organization as well as keeps up with the trustworthiness and soundness of the generally speaking monetary framework.

7. **Monetary Consideration and Availability**

The tech advancement in banking isn't just about taking care of existing clients yet additionally about advancing monetary consideration. Advanced banking and fintech arrangements can contact people and networks that recently had restricted admittance to conventional financial administrations.

Portable banking and advanced wallets are instrumental in overcoming any issues for the unbanked and underbanked populaces. These people, frequently living in remote or underserved regions, can now get to fundamental monetary administrations, make installments, and set aside cash through computerized stages.

This expanded openness advances monetary consideration, works on financial open doors, and decreases monetary variations.

Chapter 1

Historical Overview Of Banking

Banking, the act of offering monetary types of assistance, is an essential piece of mankind's set of experiences. It has advanced over centuries, adjusting to the consistently changing necessities of social orders, innovations, and financial frameworks. This verifiable outline of banking will take you on an excursion through time, following the starting points of banking, its development through different civilizations, the rise of present day financial frameworks, and the troublesome effect of innovation on the business.

The Beginning of Banking in Antiquated Times

In this part, we'll investigate the earliest types of banking that arose in antiquated developments. From the sanctuary banks of old Mesopotamia to the Roman financial frameworks and the middle age European moneylenders, we'll uncover the simple financial practices that established the groundwork for current banking.

Mesopotamian Sanctuary Banks: The support of human progress, Mesopotamia, was home to sanctuary banks where clerics assumed the part of early brokers. These organizations put away important products and offered monetary types of assistance, including loaning and record-keeping.

Roman Banking: The Romans presented the idea of trustee media, which laid the preparation for current financial practices. Roman banks worked with cash evolving, moves, and credit tasks.

Archaic Banking: Middle age Europe saw the development of moneylenders and early types of banking organizations. The Knights Knight, for instance, offered a type of worldwide banking and made the primary checks.

The Introduction of Current Banking in Renaissance Italy

The Renaissance time frame in Italy was an extraordinary period for banking. We will investigate the introduction of present day financial practices and how Italian city-states established the groundwork for the advanced financial framework.

Medici Bank: The Medici family's financial undertakings are a great representation of Renaissance-time banking. Their global organization, advancements in bookkeeping, and making of current financial practices set up for the improvement of banking establishments in Europe.

Bills of Trade: The utilization of bills of trade worked with exchange and presented the idea of credit. These monetary instruments, which looked like cutting edge checks, assumed a vital part in the extension of banking.

The Advancement of Banking Establishments in Early Present day Europe

During the early present day time frame, banking organizations started to take conspicuous structures. This section dives into the foundation of national banks, joint-stock banks, and the reconciliation of banking administrations into the more extensive economy.

Bank of Britain: The making of the Bank of Britain in 1694 denoted the introduction of present day focal banking. It presented the issuance of banknotes, giving the public a more helpful type of money.

Joint-Stock Banks: The ascent of joint-stock banks considered a more extensive dispersion of capital, empowering the funding of enormous scope modern and business undertakings.

Modern Transformation: The Modern Upheaval changed economies, prompting expanded interest for banking administrations. Banks started to offer credits to industrialists and business visionaries, encouraging monetary development.

Banking in the US

The US has a special financial history that developed in lined up with the nation's turn of events. This section centers around the foundation of the U.S. banking framework, including the job of the First and Second Banks of the US, the free financial period, and the Public Financial Framework.

First and Second Banks of the US: The Primary Bank (1791-1811) and Second Bank (1816-1836) were vital in molding the early U.S. economy, giving a steady cash and managing state-sanctioned banks.

Free Financial Period: The 1830s and 1840s saw the multiplication of state-sanctioned banks under a framework known as "free banking." These banks gave their own banknotes, prompting changing degrees of monetary solidness.

Public Financial Framework: The Public Financial Framework, laid out during the Nationwide conflict, planned to make a uniform cash and carry dependability to the financial framework.

The Economic crisis of the early 20s and the Introduction of Present day Guideline

The Economic crisis of the early 20s of the 1930s significantly affected the financial business. In this part, we'll investigate how the monetary emergency prompted the foundation of key administrative measures, including the Glass-Steagall Act and the Government Store Protection Company (FDIC).

Glass-Steagall Act: The Glass-Steagall Demonstration of 1933 isolated business banking from venture banking, meaning to forestall unsafe monetary hypothesis and irreconcilable circumstances.

Government Store Protection Partnership (FDIC): The production of the FDIC gave a wellbeing net to contributors, guaranteeing the security of their bank stores.

Banking in the Late twentieth 100 years and Then some

The last 50% of the twentieth century carried huge changes to the financial business, including the improvement of electronic banking, the ascent of worldwide banks, and the effect of globalization.

Electronic Banking: The presentation of Computerized Teller Machines (ATMs), electronic assets move, and internet banking upset the manner in which individuals got to and dealt with their funds.

Liberation and Globalization: Liberation measures, for example, the cancelation of the Glass-Steagall Act in 1999, permitted banks to differentiate their administrations, prompting the ascent of monetary aggregates and worldwide banking.

The Advanced Upheaval and the Fate of Banking

The advanced unrest in banking has changed the business, prompting the rise of online banks, fintech new companies, blockchain innovation, and the potential for national bank computerized monetary standards (CBDCs). This part investigates the effect of innovation on banking and the possible future turns of events.

Fintech Disturbance: Fintech organizations have presented inventive monetary administrations, including distributed loaning, robo-consultants, and computerized wallets, testing conventional banks.

Blockchain and Digital currency: The appearance of blockchain innovation and cryptographic forms of money like Bitcoin can possibly reshape the monetary area.

National Bank Computerized Monetary standards (CBDCs): Numerous national banks are investigating the issuance of CBDCs, which could upset how cash is given and executed.

1.1Early Banking Practices

The historical backdrop of banking is a story that unfurls across centuries, incorporating the brilliant acts of old civilizations, the spearheading endeavors of middle age moneylenders, and the early indications of current financial frameworks. These early financial practices established the groundwork for the complex monetary frameworks we have today. In this investigation, we'll travel through time, from the sanctuary banks of antiquated Mesopotamia to the appearance of the Medici Bank in Renaissance Italy, and look at what these practices meant for the course of banking history.

The Starting points of Banking in Antiquated Mesopotamia

The account of banking starts in the support of human progress, Mesopotamia, with the rise of the principal simple financial practices around 2000 BCE. During this period, sanctuaries held a focal job in the financial and public activity of the locale. The sanctuary ministers accepted the jobs of early investors, and they created monetary frameworks that worked with exchange and agrarian undertakings.

Sanctuary Banks: Sanctuaries in Mesopotamia filled in as secure storehouses for important items, including grains, materials, and valuable metals. This made them ideal spots for the supervision of abundance.

Monetary Administrations: Sanctuary banks gave advances, worked as overseers of important resources, and recorded exchanges. They likewise gave earth tablets that filled in as early types of promissory notes, permitting individuals to manage monetary exchanges without the need to convey weighty wares.

Arrangement of Trust: Sanctuary banks worked on a groundwork of trust, as they were viewed as respectable organizations. This trust permitted them to deal with monetary issues for the benefit of people and work with exchange for a great scope.

Roman Banking and the Advancement of Monetary Administrations

The Roman Domain assumed a critical part in the improvement of early financial practices. As one of the world's most memorable superpowers, it presented the idea of guardian media, laying the basis for current financial practices. The Roman financial framework changed the method for managing monetary exchanges, and it started to look like current banking in more than one way.

Guardian Media: The Romans presented the idea of trustee media. This was a type of cash that depended on trust instead of inborn worth, for example, coins made of valuable metals. The utilization of guardian media worked with greater exchange and facilitated monetary exchanges.

Roman Banks: Roman banks went about as middle people for monetary exchanges and the trading of money. They worked under the standard of trust and were instrumental in the development of the Roman economy.

Banking Houses: Banking houses, known as argentarii, arose as key foundations for monetary administrations. They gave cash evolving, moves, and credit tasks that permitted people and organizations to participate in exchange and business.

Archaic Banking and the Knights Knight

Middle age Europe saw the rise of moneylenders and early financial practices, which prepared for additional complex monetary frameworks. One of the most popular instances of early banking in this period was the Knights Knight, a strict military request.

Knights Knight: The Knights Knight, established during the twelfth hundred years, took part in a type of global banking. They worked an organization of branches all through Europe and the Blessed Land. Voyagers and pioneers could store their cash with the Knights at one area and pull out it at another, making significant distance monetary exchanges more advantageous.

Early Financial Instruments: The Knights Knight gave early types of checks, composed guarantees for installment. These really looks at empowered investors to get to their assets at any of the Knight's branches, like the cutting edge idea of a bank draft.

Mystery and Trust: The Knights laid out a standing for dependability, caution, and security, characteristics that pulled in contributors. Their practices feature the significance of confidence in early banking.

Renaissance Italy and the Introduction of Current Banking

The Renaissance time frame in Italy denoted a critical defining moment in financial history, as it saw the introduction of present day financial practices. The Italian city-states, especially Florence, became center points of monetary development and the origination of spearheading banking foundations.

Medici Bank: The Medici Bank, established by the Medici family in Florence in the fifteenth hundred years, was a milestone throughout the entire existence of banking. This bank presented new monetary practices, developments in bookkeeping, and key financial administrations that would impact the cutting edge financial framework.

Twofold Section Accounting: The Medici Bank added to the improvement of twofold passage accounting, a framework that changed monetary record-keeping. This development improved precision and straightforwardness in monetary exchanges.

Current Financial Administrations: The Medici Bank offered a great many administrations, including store accounts, credits, cash moves, unfamiliar trade, and promissory notes. It really established the groundwork for the advanced financial foundations we know today.

The Development of Early Financial Practices in Early Current Europe

During the early present day time frame, banking organizations started to take conspicuous structures. This section investigates the foundation of national banks, joint-stock banks, and the coordination of banking administrations into the more extensive economy.

Bank of Britain: The formation of the Bank of Britain in 1694 denoted the introduction of current focal banking. This organization presented the issuance of banknotes, giving the public a more helpful type of money.

Joint-Stock Banks: The ascent of joint-stock banks considered a more extensive conveyance of capital, empowering the funding of huge scope modern and business undertakings.

Modern Transformation: The Modern Upset changed economies, prompting expanded interest for banking administrations. Banks started to offer credits to industrialists and business visionaries, cultivating financial development.

1.2Evolution of Banking Services

Banking administrations have gone through a noteworthy change throughout the long term, adjusting to the changing requirements of social orders, innovations, and financial frameworks. This development follows its foundations from straightforward trade frameworks and crude loaning practices to the refined, innovation driven monetary administrations we have today. In this investigation, we'll take an excursion through time, looking at the development of banking administrations and the significant advancements that have reshaped the business.

Bargain and Crude Financial Administrations

Banking administrations, in their most simple structure, can be followed back to the deal framework and straightforward loaning rehearses. These early frameworks, which arose before the idea of cash, laid the preparation for additional complex monetary administrations.

Deal and Ware Cash: Before the innovation of money, people depended on trade to trade labor and products. Early "banks" may have been storage facilities for important wares, like grains or animals, working with trades.

Crude Loaning: As social orders developed, so did the requirement for loaning and acquiring. In these early "banking" frameworks, people could give credits of products or domesticated animals in return for revenue.

The Rise of Money and the Introduction of Essential Financial Administrations

The presentation of money denoted a significant second in the development of banking administrations. The utilization of normalized cash worked with exchange and considered more refined monetary exchanges.

Cash Frameworks: The change from bargain to money achieved the main simple financial administrations, like safe stockpiling and trade of important coins.

Moneylenders: Early moneylenders gave essential financial administrations by offering advances, recording exchanges, and frequently filling in as mediators for monetary trades.

Middle age Banking Administrations and the Ascent of Goldsmiths

During the middle age time frame, banking administrations started to take on a more organized structure. Goldsmiths and their goldsmith banks assumed a critical part in the improvement of early banking.

Goldsmiths as Brokers: Goldsmiths in archaic Europe gave secure capacity to important things, including coins and valuable metals. They gave receipts as evidence of store, really presenting the idea of banknotes.

Banking Administrations for the Affluent: Early goldsmith banks essentially took special care of the rich. They offered secure capacity, cash trade, and credit offices.

Improvement of the Check: The utilization of receipts gave by goldsmiths as a type of installment prompted the advancement of checks, perhaps of the most getting through monetary instrument throughout the entire existence of banking.

Renaissance Banking and the Introduction of Present day Financial Administrations

The Renaissance time frame in Italy saw the introduction of current financial practices, with the development of organizations like the Medici Bank. These banks presented creative administrations and established the groundwork for the financial administrations we know today.

The Medici Bank: The Medici Bank, established in the fifteenth 100 years in Florence, was instrumental in the advancement of current financial administrations.

It offered a great many administrations, including store accounts, credits, unfamiliar trade, and promissory notes.

Twofold Passage Accounting: The Medici Bank added to the improvement of twofold section accounting, a framework that reformed monetary record-keeping. This advancement upgraded exactness and straightforwardness in monetary exchanges.

Advancement in Global Banking: The Renaissance period saw the ascent of worldwide banking and the utilization of bills of trade, which considered the effective exchange of assets and worked with significant distance exchange.

Early Present day Banking and the Ascent of Joint-Stock Banks

The early current time frame saw the foundation of national banks, joint-stock banks, and the combination of banking administrations into the more extensive economy.

Bank of Britain: The Bank of Britain, laid out in 1694, was a critical achievement in early present day banking. It denoted the introduction of present day focal banking and presented the issuance of banknotes, giving a more helpful type of cash for people in general.

Joint-Stock Banks: The ascent of joint-stock banks considered a more extensive conveyance of capital. This advancement empowered the funding of huge scope modern and business endeavors.

Modern Insurgency and Banking: The Modern Transformation changed economies, expanding the interest for banking administrations. Banks started to offer credits to industrialists and business people, encouraging financial development.

twentieth Century Banking Administrations and Guideline

The twentieth century carried massive changes to banking administrations, with the extension of buyer banking, the advancement of current installment frameworks, and the execution of administrative measures.

Shopper Banking: The twentieth century saw the extension of purchaser banking, as banks offered a great many administrations to individual clients, including investment accounts, individual credits, and home loan funding.

Current Installment Frameworks: The advancement of electronic banking, Visas, and the broad utilization of Computerized Teller Machines (ATMs) altered how individuals got to and dealt with their funds.

Administrative Measures: The twentieth century saw the execution of urgent administrative measures, for example, the Glass-Steagall Act and the foundation of store protection programs like the Government Store Protection Organization (FDIC) in the US.

The Advanced Transformation and the Eventual fate of Banking Administrations

The computerized unrest in banking has changed the business, prompting the development of online banks, fintech new companies, blockchain innovation, and the potential for national bank advanced monetary standards (CBDCs).

Fintech Disturbance: Fintech organizations have presented imaginative monetary administrations, including distributed loaning, robo-counselors, and computerized wallets, testing conventional banks.

Blockchain and Cryptographic money: The appearance of blockchain innovation and digital currencies like Bitcoin can possibly reshape the monetary area.

National Bank Computerized Monetary standards (CBDCs): Numerous national banks are investigating the issuance of CBDCs, which could alter how cash is given and executed.

1.3Technological Milestones in Banking

The financial business has gone through a huge change throughout the course of recent many years, because of ceaseless progressions in innovation. These innovative achievements have reclassified the manner in which monetary establishments work, offering clients more prominent comfort and availability while at the same time working on functional productivity and security. In this article, we will investigate the crucial mechanical achievements in banking, following their advancement and effect on the business. From the earliest advancements like ATMs to the most recent improvements in blockchain and computerized reasoning, this excursion through the chronicles of banking innovation uncovers the complicated and dynamic connection among money and innovation.

The Approach of the Robotized Teller Machine (ATM)

The Mechanized Teller Machine, or ATM, is much of the time thought about the primary major mechanical achievement in banking. Developed by John Shepherd-Barron and presented by Barclays in 1967, the ATM altered client admittance to cash. It permitted bank clients to pull out cash, check their record adjusts, and put aside installments day in and day out, no matter what a branch's working hours. ATMs are presently omnipresent around the world, offering phenomenal accommodation to purchasers and lessening the requirement for actual bank offices. Throughout the long term, ATMs have advanced to offer more functionalities, for example, bill installments, account moves, and even really look at stores.

The Ascent of Internet Banking

The appearance of the web in the late twentieth century achieved one more huge achievement in financial innovation - web based banking. Web based banking permits clients to get to their records, view exchange history, move assets, and even apply for advances from the solace of their homes or workplaces.

This shift towards computerized banking denoted a significant decrease in the dependence on actual bank offices and paper-based exchanges. It likewise empowered banks to smooth out their tasks and proposition more cutthroat items and administrations.

Portable Banking and the Multiplication of Cell phones

As cell phones acquired fame, portable banking arose as a unique advantage in the financial business. The far and wide reception of cell phones permitted clients to convey their banks in their pockets. Portable banking applications give a scope of administrations, including account the board, versatile stores, and asset moves. They additionally presented highlights like biometric validation and pop-up messages for improved security and client experience. This achievement made financial more open, helpful, and customized for clients, essentially decreasing the requirement for in-person financial administrations.

Electronic Assets Move and Installment Frameworks

Electronic Assets Move (EFT) frameworks assumed a urgent part in changing how cash is moved inside the financial biological system. EFT frameworks work with the exchange of assets starting with one record then onto the next electronically, taking into account quicker, safer exchanges. The advancement of Mechanized Clearing Houses (ACH) in the US and comparative frameworks overall worked with electronic exchanges, including direct store of pay rates, electronic bill installments, and interbank reserve moves. These frameworks made ready for present day installment advances, including wire moves, computerized wallets, and shared installment stages.

The Rise of Charge and Mastercards

Charge and Visas upset how individuals make installments and access reserves. While the idea of Visas traces all the way back to the 1920s, their boundless use and electronic handling altogether changed banking. Charge cards, which consider direct admittance to the client's checking or investment account, acquired prevalence as a helpful installment strategy. Charge cards, then again, offered a credit extension, empowering customers to make buys with acquired cash and reimburse it later. The reconciliation of attractive stripe innovation and, later, EMV chips improved the security of these cards.

Web Banking and the Extension of Online Administrations

Web banking, frequently alluded to as e-banking or e-banking administrations, addresses a continuation of the web based financial development.

Web banking not just gives essential record data and asset move capacities yet additionally permits clients to go through with additional complex monetary exchanges, like stock exchanging and overseeing speculation portfolios. This development of administrations online made it more straightforward for clients to deal with their funds and speculation exercises from the solace of their homes.

Advanced Wallets and Contactless Installments

Computerized wallets, for example, Mac Pay, Google Pay, and Samsung Pay, denoted a huge achievement in banking and installment innovations. These versatile applications store clients' installment card data, permitting them to make contactless installments utilizing their cell phones or smartwatches. Computerized wallets have become progressively famous, particularly following the Coronavirus pandemic, as they offer a more sterile and helpful method for making exchanges. Also, these wallets frequently support faithfulness and prize projects, making them considerably more interesting to buyers.

Blockchain and Digital money

The presentation of blockchain innovation through Bitcoin in 2009 started a significant change in the monetary business. Blockchain is a decentralized, conveyed record innovation that supports digital forms of money and can possibly reform conventional financial cycles. The utilization of blockchain offers more prominent security, straightforwardness, and effectiveness in monetary exchanges. Digital forms of money like Bitcoin, Ethereum, and others have acquired notoriety as elective types of advanced resources, provoking conventional monetary frameworks and prompting the development of cryptographic money trades and decentralized finance (DeFi) stages.

Man-made brainpower (artificial intelligence) and AI

Man-made brainpower (artificial intelligence) and AI (ML) have changed banking through mechanization, information investigation, and further developed client assistance. Man-made intelligence controlled chatbots and remote helpers give continuous client care, addressing requests and helping with exchanges. AI calculations investigate immense datasets to identify misrepresentation, anticipate market drifts, and customize monetary administrations. Artificial intelligence is likewise utilized for risk appraisal in loaning and speculation choices, adding to the advancement of robo-guides that oversee venture portfolios with negligible human mediation.

Administrative Innovation (RegTech)

Administrative innovation, or RegTech, is a subset of fintech that spotlights on assisting monetary foundations with conforming to complex administrative prerequisites. As guidelines in the financial area turned out to be more rigid and requesting, RegTech arose to improve and smooth out the consistence cycle. Innovations, for example, blockchain, computer based intelligence, and information investigation are utilized to screen and give an account of monetary exercises, identify likely extortion, and guarantee that banks comply to administrative rules. RegTech arrangements assume a significant part in diminishing the expense of consistence and moderating gamble in the financial business.

Open Banking and PSD2

Open Banking is a drive that urges monetary organizations to impart client information to approved outsider suppliers through Application Programming Points of interaction (APIs). The European Association's Installment Administrations Mandate 2 (PSD2) guideline assumed a vital part in driving the reception of Open Banking. Open Banking empowers clients to get to a more extensive scope of monetary items and administrations, including account conglomeration, planning devices, and inventive installment arrangements presented by outsider suppliers. This achievement advances rivalry and encourages development inside the financial area.

Distributed computing

Distributed computing has turned into a fundamental piece of current financial foundation. By moving information and applications to the cloud, banks can lessen functional expenses, further develop adaptability, and improve information security. The cloud additionally takes into account the quick organization of new administrations and applications, making it more straightforward for banks to adjust to changing client requests and administrative necessities. Cloud innovation upholds on the web and portable banking, information investigation, and chance administration, among other basic financial capabilities.

Network protection Headways

As innovation develops, so do the dangers to the financial business. Banks have put altogether in network safety to safeguard client information and monetary resources. High level safety efforts, for example, multifaceted confirmation, biometric acknowledgment (unique mark, facial acknowledgment, and iris examining), and computerized reasoning for peculiarity location, have become norm in banking. These developments assist with defending monetary data and exchanges during a time of expanding digital dangers.

Moment Installments

Moment installment frameworks, for example, the Single Euro Installments Region Moment Credit Move (SEPA Moment), have carried constant exchanges to the front line of the financial business. These frameworks empower people and organizations to make installments that are handled in no time, upgrading the speed and accommodation of monetary exchanges. Moment installments are a reaction to the interest for quicker and more productive installment arrangements, offering an option in contrast to conventional, more slow settlement processes.

Monetary Consideration and Versatile Banking in Agricultural Nations

Mechanical achievements in banking are not restricted to created countries. Versatile banking plays had a urgent impact in advancing monetary consideration in arising and creating economies. In locales with restricted admittance to customary financial foundation, portable financial stages have turned into a fundamental apparatus for overseeing funds, making installments, and getting to credit. This achievement has fundamentally worked on monetary access and financial open doors for a large number of individuals around the world.

Quantum Figuring

While still in its beginning phases, quantum figuring can possibly change the financial area. Quantum PCs can handle huge measures of information at speeds right now incomprehensible with traditional PCs. This innovation holds the commitment of taking care of mind boggling monetary issues, for example, improving portfolios, risk evaluation, and extortion identification, at a degree of accuracy and proficiency that was beforehand out of reach.

Decentralized Money (DeFi)

Decentralized Money, or DeFi, addresses a new mechanical achievement that has earned huge consideration. DeFi stages work on blockchain innovation and offer monetary types of assistance, like loaning, getting, exchanging, and yield cultivating, without middle people like conventional banks. These stages offer clients the amazing chance to take part in an open and permissionless monetary biological system, upsetting the customary financial model. While DeFi holds extraordinary commitment, it likewise presents administrative and security challenges.

Chapter 2

The Digital Revolution

The Computerized Insurgency, otherwise called the Third Modern Transformation, is a characterizing element of the 21st hundred years. It has achieved an extraordinary change by they way we live, work, convey, and direct business. Not at all like past modern upsets, which were portrayed by mechanical and simple advancements, the Computerized Upheaval is driven by computerized innovations, programming, and the web. In this complete investigation, we will dive into the multi-layered elements of the Computerized Upheaval, its verifiable setting, its effect on different parts of society, and the open doors and difficulties it presents.

Grasping the Computerized Unrest

The Computerized Transformation addresses the progress from simple, mechanical, and electronic advancements to advanced innovations, which depend on discrete twofold code (0s and 1s). It incorporates a great many progressions, including the turn of events and expansion of PCs, the web, cell phones, virtual entertainment, distributed computing, enormous information examination, computerized reasoning, and the Web of Things (IoT). These advanced innovations have not just improved our capacity to process and share data yet have likewise impacted the manner in which we live and collaborate with the world.

Authentic Setting: The Development of Innovation

To see the value in the meaning of the Computerized Unrest, it is vital to comprehend its authentic setting and how it fits inside the more extensive structure of mechanical advancement. All things considered, mechanical progressions have happened in a few unmistakable stages, known as modern upheavals:

The Main Modern Transformation (late eighteenth hundred years): This unrest was set apart by the change from agrarian economies to modern economies, driven by motorization, the improvement of the steam motor, and the presentation of production line frameworks.

The Second Modern Transformation (late nineteenth to mid twentieth 100 years): This period saw the multiplication of electrical power, the innovation of the phone, the development of the steel business, and the approach of the gas powered motor.

The Third Modern Insurgency (late twentieth 100 years to the present): This is the Advanced Unrest, described by the ascent of computerized innovations, individualized computing, and the web.The Advanced Transformation expands on the establishments laid by the initial two modern upsets, however it is remarkable in its ability to reshape each part of present day life.

Key Parts of the Computerized Transformation

The Computerized Unrest is multi-layered and envelops a wide exhibit of parts. Here are a portion of the critical mechanical turns of events and developments that play had an essential impact in forming this change:

PCs: The far reaching accessibility and reasonableness of PCs were instrumental in the Computerized Upheaval. PCs enable people to get to data, convey, and make computerized content.

The Web: The web has achieved a worldwide organization that interfaces people, organizations, states, and establishments. It has altered correspondence, business, and data spread, making the world more interconnected than any other time in recent memory.

Cell phones: These pocket-sized gadgets have become universal, giving admittance to a huge swath of data and administrations. They have reformed the manner in which we impart, explore, shop, and consume media.

Online Entertainment: Stages like Facebook, Twitter, Instagram, and LinkedIn have changed the manner in which we associate, share, and collaborate with each other. Virtual entertainment has turned into an incredible asset for correspondence, publicizing, and preparing social and political developments.

Distributed computing: Cloud innovation empowers the capacity and recovery of information and programming applications over the web. It offers versatility, adaptability, and cost-effectiveness for organizations and people.

Large Information and Examination: The capacity to gather, process, and break down enormous volumes of information has upset dynamic in different fields, including medical services, money, promoting, and planned operations.

Computerized reasoning (simulated intelligence) and AI: simulated intelligence and AI calculations are utilized to robotize errands, make forecasts, and customize client encounters. They are changing enterprises like medical care, money, and transportation.

The Web of Things (IoT): IoT interfaces ordinary items to the web, permitting them to send and get information. This innovation is utilized in brilliant homes, associated vehicles, and modern applications.

Advanced Installments: Computerized installment frameworks, including cryptographic forms of money like Bitcoin, have upset conventional banking and money by empowering shared exchanges and decentralized monetary standards.

Web based business: Internet shopping has altered the manner in which customers purchase labor and products. Online business stages like Amazon, Alibaba, and eBay have developed into worldwide monsters.

Effect of the Advanced Transformation

The Advanced Transformation has significantly affected different parts of society, including financial aspects, schooling, medical care, legislative issues, correspondence, and culture. We should investigate the broad impacts of this change:

Financial Change

The Advanced Upheaval has reshaped the worldwide economy in various ways:

1. **The Ascent of Tech Goliaths:** Organizations like Apple, Amazon, Google, Facebook, and Microsoft have turned into a portion of the world's most significant partnerships, overwhelming different areas, including innovation, online business, and computerized promoting.
2. **Work Disturbance:** Computerization and digitalization have prompted work removal in specific businesses, like assembling, while at the same time setting out new position open doors in tech-related fields like programming advancement, information examination, and network protection.
3. **Web based business Development:** Internet shopping has developed dramatically, prompting the decay of customary physical retailers and the ascent of online business goliaths like Amazon.
4. **Independent and Gig Economy:** Advanced stages have worked with the ascent of the gig economy, empowering people to function as specialists or workers for hire in different fields.
5. **Fintech Advancement:** Monetary innovation (fintech) organizations have upset customary banking and money, offering administrations, for example, computerized installments, distributed loaning, and robo-consultants.

Instruction and Learning

The Advanced Unrest has changed schooling and learning in the accompanying ways:

1. **Online Instruction:** The accessibility of online courses, stages, and instructive substance has made learning more open and adaptable. Monstrous Open Internet based Courses (MOOCs) and e-learning stages have acquired prominence.
2. **Distance Learning:** The Coronavirus pandemic sped up the reception of remote and mixture getting the hang of, featuring the significance of computerized apparatuses and assets in training.

3. **Customized Learning:** computer based intelligence driven versatile learning frameworks can possibly customize instructive substance and adjust to individual understudies' necessities.

Medical services and Medication

The Computerized Upset has changed medical services and medication:

1. **Telemedicine:** Telehealth administrations and virtual discussions have become all the more generally utilized, further developing medical care availability and decreasing the requirement for in-person visits.
2. **Electronic Wellbeing Records:** Advanced wellbeing records have upgraded patient information the executives and empowered more productive and exact medical care conveyance.
3. **Clinical Diagnostics:** computer based intelligence and AI are being utilized to foster indicative apparatuses that can identify illnesses and conditions with high exactness.

Correspondence and Social Cooperation

Computerized innovation has changed the manner in which we impart and collaborate:

1. **Online Entertainment:** Virtual entertainment stages have become indispensable to how we associate with others, share data, and draw in with recent developments.
2. **Texting:** Informing applications like WhatsApp, WeChat, and Courier have swapped customary text informing for some clients.
3. **Video Conferencing:** The notoriety of video conferencing stages like Zoom and Microsoft Groups flooded during the Coronavirus pandemic, meaningfully altering the manner in which we direct conferences and parties.

Political and Social Change

The Computerized Transformation significantly affects legislative issues and social elements:

1. **Data Scattering:** Computerized stages have sped up the spread of data, permitting people to get to news and participate in friendly and political activism.
2. **Social Developments:** Virtual entertainment has been an impetus for social developments and political fights, empowering grassroots getting sorted out and bringing issues to light of significant issues.

3. **Computerized Gap:** While advanced innovation has associated individuals around the world, it has likewise featured the advanced separation, where admittance to computerized assets and abilities is inconsistent.

Social Change

Computerized innovation has reshaped culture and amusement:

1. **Real time features:** Streaming stages like Netflix, Amazon Prime, and Spotify have changed how we consume amusement, music, and video content.
2. **Advanced Workmanship and Imagination:** The Computerized Unrest has led to new types of craftsmanship, including advanced workmanship, augmented reality encounters, and computer games.
3. **Advanced Distributing:** digital books and computerized distributing have impacted the manner in which we read and access writing.

Natural Effect

The Advanced Insurgency has both positive and negative ecological impacts:

1. **Natural Checking:** IoT gadgets and computerized innovation are utilized for natural observing and the executives, assisting with tending to environmental change and biological difficulties.
2. **Electronic Waste:** The multiplication of electronic gadgets has prompted worries about electronic waste and the mindful removal of obsolete innovation.

Potential open doors and Difficulties

The Computerized Insurgency presents a scope of chances and difficulties for people, organizations, and society all in all:

Open doors:

Further developed Proficiency: Advanced innovations improve efficiency and productivity, making processes more smoothed out and financially savvy.

Admittance to Data: The web gives unmatched admittance to data and instructive assets.

Development and Inventiveness: The Computerized Unrest energizes advancement and engages people to make and share their thoughts, workmanship, and items.

Upgraded Network: Advanced specialized apparatuses empower individuals to interface across geological limits.

Financial Development: The computerized economy is a main impetus for monetary development and occupation creation.

Challenges:

Protection Concerns: The assortment and utilization of individual information by tech organizations raise worries about protection and information security.

Online protection Dangers: The interconnected idea of the advanced world makes it defenseless to cyberattacks and information breaks.

Computerized Separation: Abberations in admittance to innovation and advanced education make social and financial imbalances.

Work Relocation: Mechanization and computerized reasoning might prompt work uprooting and the requirement for reskilling.

Deception and Phony News: The quick spread of bogus or misdirecting data on computerized stages presents difficulties to informed independent direction and public talk.

Advanced Compulsion: The inescapable utilization of cell phones and virtual entertainment can prompt fixation and adversely influence emotional wellness.

2.1Emergence of Online Banking

The development of web based banking has been an extraordinary power in the monetary business, changing the manner in which people and organizations deal with their cash and cooperate with monetary foundations. Web based banking, otherwise called web banking or computerized banking, has developed from straightforward equilibrium requests to far reaching monetary administration, making it a fundamental piece of current banking. This article investigates the authentic advancement of internet banking, its effect on the monetary area, advantages, challenges, and the fate of computerized banking.

Authentic Advancement

Internet banking has a rich history, set apart by a few key achievements:

1980s-1990s: Development of Web Banking

The idea of web banking flourished in the last part of the 1980s and mid 1990s when banks started offering on the web administrations, principally for balance requests and asset moves. These early administrations were much of the time text-based and required dial-up associations.

Late 1990s: More extensive Web Reception

As web access turned out to be more inescapable, banks started to offer electronic internet banking stages. These stages gave more easy to understand interfaces, making ready for clients to lead a more extensive scope of exchanges on the web.

2000s: Development of Internet Banking Administrations

During the 2000s, web based financial administrations extended fundamentally. Clients could perform errands like bill installments, account the executives, and, surprisingly, open new records by means of online stages. Safety efforts likewise improved to construct trust among clients.

2010s: Portable Banking Arises

With the multiplication of cell phones, portable banking turned into a prevailing power in web based banking. Committed versatile applications permitted clients to deal with their funds in a hurry. This period saw the appearance of highlights like versatile stores, remote really look at catch, and distributed installment choices.

Present and Then some: Fintech Incorporation and Then some

Today, internet banking stages are complete monetary center points, frequently coordinated with fintech administrations. Clients can contribute, get credits, and access a scope of monetary instruments through their web based financial records. Man-made consciousness and AI are progressively utilized for customized suggestions and upgraded security.

Influence on the Monetary Area

The rise of internet banking significantly affects the monetary area:

Comfort and Openness

Web based banking has made it simpler for people and organizations to deal with their funds. Clients can get to their records and perform exchanges every minute of every day from the solace of their homes or in a hurry.

Cost Decrease for Banks

Web based banking altogether diminishes the expense of conventional physical banking, including staff and framework. This permits banks to give cost reserve funds to clients as lower charges and better loan fees.

Worldwide Reach

Web based banking has empowered banks to extend their arrive at past actual branch areas. This has prompted more noteworthy rivalry and advancement in the monetary area.

Fintech Joining

Web based financial stages are progressively incorporating fintech administrations, making it more straightforward for clients to get to speculation potential open doors, individual advances, and monetary administration devices.

Improved Security

While web based banking has achieved new security challenges, it has additionally prompted progressions in online protection. Banks put resources into hearty encryption, multifaceted validation, and constant misrepresentation recognition to guard client information.

Advantages of Web based Banking

Web based financial offers various advantages to the two purchasers and monetary organizations:

Comfort

Internet banking is accessible all day, every day, permitting clients to deal with their funds at whatever point it's generally advantageous for them.

Cost Reserve funds

Advanced banking diminishes the requirement for actual branches, prompting cost reserve funds for the two banks and clients.

Availability

Web based banking is available to people who might not have simple admittance to actual bank offices, remembering those for country or underserved regions.

Speed and Proficiency

Exchanges through web based banking are handled rapidly, lessening stand by times and expanding productivity.

Account The board

Clients can screen account adjusts, track exchanges, and set up account alarms to remain informed about their monetary movement.

Charge Installments and Moves

Covering bills and moving cash between accounts or to others should be possible easily through internet banking stages.

Portable Access

Portable banking applications permit clients to deal with their funds in a hurry, making it particularly helpful for occupied people.

Difficulties and Concerns

In spite of its many benefits, web based banking isn't without its difficulties and concerns:

Security Dangers

Web based banking is helpless to online protection dangers, for example, hacking and fraud. Banks put resources into hearty safety efforts, however clients should likewise avoid potential risk, for example, solid secret key practices and two-factor confirmation.

Computerized Separation

Not every person has equivalent admittance to web based banking. The advanced separation might bar a few people, especially in underserved or distant regions, from the advantages of web based banking.

Specialized Issues

Internet banking stages can encounter specialized misfires, which can be baffling for clients who depend on them for ordinary exchanges.

Protection Concerns

Internet banking includes sharing individual and monetary data web based, raising security concerns. Banks should comply with severe security guidelines to safeguard client information.

Overreliance on Innovation

Overreliance on computerized financial administrations might restrict eye to eye cooperations with bank work force, possibly affecting client connections.

Phishing and Tricks

Con artists and fraudsters utilize different strategies to fool people into uncovering their own and monetary data. Clients should stay cautious against phishing and tricks.

The Fate of Web based Banking

The eventual fate of web based banking is probably going to be formed by a few key patterns:

Improved Client Experience

Banks will keep on putting resources into easy to use interfaces, making it more straightforward for clients to explore their computerized financial stages.

Man-made reasoning (artificial intelligence)

Man-made intelligence will assume a more huge part in customizing banking encounters, offering custom-made monetary counsel, and further developing safety efforts.

Blockchain and Digital currencies

The coordination of blockchain innovation and the utilization of digital currencies might turn out to be more typical in web based banking for upgraded security and proficiency.

Advanced Character and Biometrics

Improved biometric validation strategies, for example, facial acknowledgment and unique finger impression examining, will reinforce security in web based banking.

Open Banking

Open financial drives, which take into account the sharing of monetary information among banks and outsider fintech suppliers, will keep on advancing, furnishing clients with additional choices and administrations.

Administrative Changes

Continuous administrative improvements will shape the scene of internet banking, with an emphasis on information protection and monetary security.

Monetary Consideration

Endeavors to connect the computerized separation will keep, guaranteeing that web based financial administrations are open to a more extensive populace.

2.2The Role of ATMs

Computerized Teller Machines (ATMs) have turned into a necessary piece of current banking, offering unrivaled comfort, openness, and many monetary administrations to clients. ATMs have developed essentially since their beginning and keep on assuming a critical part in the realm of banking.

In this article, we will analyze the multi-layered job of ATMs, their authentic advancement, the effect they have on clients and the financial business, as well as the difficulties and future possibilities they face.

The Introduction of ATMs

The idea of Mechanized Teller Machines was conceived out of the requirement for more noteworthy comfort in banking. The world's most memorable fruitful ATM was presented by Barclays Bank in London in 1967. This early machine permitted clients to pull out cash beyond normal financial hours, denoting a huge takeoff from customary financial practices. It established the groundwork for an unrest in financial administrations.

The Job of ATMs in Banking

ATMs serve a large number of fundamental jobs in current banking:

Cash Withdrawals: The essential capability of ATMs is to furnish clients with admittance to their money whenever, anyplace. This capacity has altogether diminished the requirement for people to visit actual bank offices for straightforward exchanges, offering every minute of every day accessibility.

Stores: Numerous ATMs currently permit clients to store registers and money straightforwardly with their records. This has smoothed out the store interaction, giving a fast and helpful way for clients to add assets to their records without visiting a bank employee.

Balance Requests: ATMs give clients continuous admittance to their record adjusts. Clients can without much of a stretch really look at their monetary status, screen exchanges, and track their spending.

Store Moves: A few ATMs empower clients to move assets between accounts, cover bills, and start other monetary exchanges, making them flexible instruments for overseeing funds.

Money and Really look at Advances: ATMs offer the choice for clients to demand loans using a credit card and charge cards. Furthermore, they can be utilized to cash checks, lessening the requirement for people to visit banks for these administrations.

Little Explanations: Numerous ATMs offer the comfort of printing smaller than usual proclamations that sum up ongoing record exchanges, furnishing clients with a speedy outline of their monetary movement.

The Development of ATMs

ATMs have gone through critical development since their beginning:

Fundamental Exchanges to Complete Administrations: While early ATMs basically administered cash, current ATMs offer an extensive scope of administrations, including stores, bill installments, balance requests, and, surprisingly, the capacity to buy pre-loaded cards.

Upgraded Security: Security has turned into a central worry for ATMs. They are presently outfitted with cutting edge safety efforts, like scrambled exchanges, against skimming innovation, and ongoing extortion identification, to safeguard clients and their exchanges.

Incorporation with Portable Banking: Many banks have coordinated their ATMs with versatile banking applications, permitting clients to organize exchanges through their cell phones and complete them at the ATM, upgrading accommodation and security.

Worldwide Openness: ATMs have developed into a worldwide organization, permitting clients to get to their records and pull out cash in different nations utilizing their house bank's ATMs. This furnishes voyagers with advantageous admittance to their assets around the world.

Multi-Cash Backing: In regions with high worldwide the travel industry, a few ATMs currently support multi-money withdrawals, empowering voyagers to handily get unfamiliar money.

Cash Reusing: Money reusing ATMs, which acknowledge and apportion similar notes, have decreased the requirement for actual money transportation, bringing about cost reserve funds for banks and expanded accommodation for clients.

Biometric Confirmation: A few ATMs utilize biometric verification strategies, for example, unique finger impression or iris sweeps to improve security and decrease dependence on customary PINs.

Influence on Clients

ATMs significantly affect clients and their financial encounters:

Comfort: ATMs give unrivaled accommodation by offering day in and day out admittance to monetary administrations, permitting clients to pull out cash, set aside installments, and complete different exchanges whenever it might suit them.

Decreased Dependence on Branches: The accessibility of ATMs has essentially diminished the requirement for clients to visit actual bank offices for routine exchanges, saving time and lessening the need to stand by in teller lines.

More extensive Availability: ATMs have extended financial openness, empowering account holders to get to their assets in different areas, including distant regions where actual bank offices might be scant.

More prominent Command Over Funds: ATMs permit clients to screen their record adjusts and late exchanges, giving better command over their funds.

Protection and Independence: ATMs offer a degree of security and independence in banking. Clients can pull out money and manage exchanges without expecting to communicate with bank work force.

Difficulties and Concerns

While ATMs bring various advantages, they additionally accompany difficulties and concerns:

Security Dangers: ATMs are helpless to different security dangers, including card skimming, card catching, and actual robbery. Banks put vigorously in safety efforts to safeguard their ATMs and clients.

Upkeep and Margin time: ATMs require standard support, and specialized issues can prompt margin time. This can be baffling for clients who depend on ATMs for their financial requirements.

Misrepresentation and Tricks: Con artists have created different strategies to target ATM clients, including phishing assaults and the utilization of false card-understanding gadgets.

Cash Deficiencies: In certain districts, ATMs might encounter cash deficiencies or blackouts, restricting admittance to cash for clients.

The Fate of ATMs

ATMs keep on being a basic part of current banking, and their future looks encouraging:

Cutting edge innovation: ATMs will keep on embracing trend setting innovations, like contactless card perusers, biometric validation, and upgraded security highlights.

Multi-Usefulness: ATMs will grow their scope of administrations, possibly including more complicated exchanges like advance applications and record openings.

Supportability: Endeavors are being made to lessen the natural effect of ATMs through energy-proficient plans and money reusing.

Mix with Versatile Banking: ATMs will keep on coordinating with portable banking applications, taking into account consistent and secure exchanges started through cell phones.

Worldwide Network: The worldwide reach of ATMs will extend, giving voyagers significantly more noteworthy admittance to their assets around the world.

2.3Internet Banking and Its Impact

Web banking, otherwise called internet banking or e-banking, has changed the manner in which individuals collaborate with their banks and deal with their funds. This computerized development has made financial more helpful as well as significantly affected the whole monetary scene. In this article, we'll investigate web banking, its advancement, the advantages it offers, its effect on clients and customary banking, and the difficulties it stances to the monetary business.

The Advancement of Web Banking

Web banking has a generally short yet wonderful history. Its underlying foundations can be followed back to the 1980s, yet it built up momentum during the 1990s as the web turned out to be all the more broadly open.

From the outset, internet banking was restricted to essential undertakings like financial records adjusts and moving assets. Nonetheless, the 21st century saw the fast development of web banking, with banks presenting a wide cluster of administrations, including bill installments, credit applications, speculation the board, and that's only the tip of the iceberg. Portable banking applications further extended the capacities of web banking, permitting clients to deal with their funds in a hurry.

The Job of Web Banking

Web banking assumes a diverse part in the monetary area:

Accommodation and Openness: Web banking permits clients to get to their records and perform different exchanges from the solace of their homes, workplaces, or even while voyaging. It gives all day, every day accessibility, wiping out the need to stick to customary financial hours.

Proficiency and Speed: Web banking decreases the time and exertion expected for routine monetary undertakings. Clients can move reserves, cover bills, and, surprisingly, open new records with only a couple of snaps.

Cost Decrease: For the two clients and banks, web banking lessens the expenses related with customary banking, like the requirement for broad actual framework and faculty.

Worldwide Reach: Web banking empowers clients to manage monetary exchanges no matter what their geological area. It has extended financial availability, dispensing with the limitations of actual branch areas.

Reconciliation with Fintech: Web banking stages frequently coordinate with fintech administrations, permitting clients to get to speculation open doors, individual credits, and monetary administration devices inside a similar stage.

Improved Security: With progressions in network safety, web banking has become progressively secure, safeguarding client information through encryption, multifaceted validation, and ongoing misrepresentation location.

Influence on Clients

Web banking significantly affects clients:

Comfort and Control: Clients can deal with their funds whenever it might suit them, from anyplace with a web association. This adaptability gives a feeling of command over their monetary issues.

Time and Cost Reserve funds: Web banking diminishes the requirement for actual visits to bank offices, saving time and possibly bringing down expenses related with customary financial administrations.

Admittance to A great many Administrations: Clients can play out a far reaching set of banking undertakings on the web, from really looking at balances to applying for credits, money management, and in any event, buying protection.

Customization and Personalization: Web banking stages use client information and man-made intelligence to offer customized monetary exhortation, item suggestions, and custom-made client encounters.

Decreased Administrative work: Many financial cycles, like record articulations, have progressed to computerized designs, diminishing the requirement for paper documentation.

Influence on Conventional Banking

Web banking has tested conventional banking in more ways than one:

Branch Significance: As clients progressively go to web banking, the importance of actual bank offices has lessened. Many banks have needed to reexamine their branch organizations and administrations.

Reception of Computerized Advancements: Customary banks have needed to put resources into advanced innovations and work on their internet based contributions to rival online-just banks and fintech new businesses.

Cost Change: While web banking diminishes specific functional expenses, it likewise requires interests in online protection and advanced foundation, which customary banks have needed to adjust to.

Change in Client Communication: The connection among banks and clients is moving from face to face associations to advanced and remote channels.

Rivalry from Fintech: Fintech organizations offering on the web just monetary administrations have arisen as imposing contenders to customary banks.

Difficulties and Concerns

Regardless of its various benefits, web banking likewise presents a few difficulties and concerns:

Security Dangers: The computerized idea of web banking opens clients to different security dangers, including phishing, data fraud, and hacking. Banks should keep up with powerful safety efforts and teach clients on prescribed procedures.

Advanced Education: Not all clients have a similar degree of computerized proficiency, which can prompt differences in their capacity to get to and use web based financial administrations.

Client care: The shift to advanced channels has diminished eye to eye communications, affecting client connections and the capacity to offer customized help.

Security Concerns: Web banking expects clients to share individual and monetary data web based, raising worries about information protection and its insurance.

Free time and Specialized Issues: Specialized errors and framework margin time can thwart the internet banking experience, making disappointment for clients.

Computerized Separation: Not every person has equivalent admittance to the web and web fit gadgets, bringing about a computerized partition that can restrict monetary incorporation.

The Fate of Web Banking

The eventual fate of web banking is probably going to be molded by a few key patterns:

Trend setting innovation: Web banking stages will keep on taking on cutting edge innovations, for example, man-made consciousness and AI, to offer more customized types of assistance and upgraded security.

Versatile Driven Insight: With the rising utilization of cell phones, web banking will put a more grounded accentuation on portable applications, guaranteeing that clients can deal with their funds in a hurry.

Open Banking: Open financial drives will keep on developing, empowering clients to get to a more extensive scope of monetary administrations and coordinate different monetary items into a solitary stage.

Blockchain and Digital currencies: The coordination of blockchain innovation and the utilization of cryptographic forms of money might turn out to be more normal in web banking, offering improved security and effectiveness.

Administrative Changes: Progressing administrative improvements will shape the scene of web banking, with an emphasis on information protection, monetary security, and customer insurance.

2.4The Birth of Mobile Banking

Portable banking, frequently alluded to as "m-banking," has arisen as a progressive power in the monetary business. It permits people to get to their financial balances, go through with exchanges, and deal with their funds through cell phones like cell phones and tablets. In this article, we'll investigate the birth and advancement of versatile banking, its effect on the monetary area, advantages, challenges, and the job it plays in our undeniably digitalized world.

The Introduction of Versatile Banking

The idea of portable banking started to come to fruition in the mid 2000s, with the approach of cell phones with web network. The principal portable financial administrations were essential and fundamentally centered around giving clients data like record adjusts and exchange history. Be that as it may, the genuine birth of portable banking can be followed to the presentation of versatile applications and further developed versatile web foundation.

The defining moment accompanied the arrival of the iPhone in 2007, which denoted a huge change in how individuals cooperated with their cell phones. The blend of cell phones and devoted versatile banking applications made a fruitful ground for portable banking to flourish. Before long, monetary organizations started to foster easy to use applications that permitted clients to play out an extensive variety of banking errands on their cell phones, from financial records adjusts to moving assets, taking care of bills, and in any event, exchanging stocks.

The Job of Portable Banking

Portable banking has changed the manner in which people and organizations collaborate with their banks and manage monetary exchanges:

day in and day out Access: One of the main benefits of versatile banking is the capacity to get to monetary data and manage exchanges whenever and from anyplace with a web association. This nonstop accessibility has made financial administrations more advantageous.

Comfort and Speed: Portable banking smoothes out monetary undertakings, dispensing with the need to visit an actual branch. Clients can move reserves, cover bills, store checks, and perform other financial exercises with a couple of taps on their cell phones.

Monetary Administration: Versatile banking applications frequently incorporate elements for planning, cost following, and venture the board, assisting clients with keeping steady over their monetary objectives.

Upgraded Security: Versatile banking applications consolidate strong safety efforts, including biometric verification (unique finger impression or facial acknowledgment), encryption, and multifaceted confirmation, to safeguard clients' delicate monetary data.

Account Alarms: Portable banking applications permit clients to set up account cautions and notices, for example, exchange alarms, low equilibrium admonitions, or security cautions, keeping them informed about their monetary movement.

The Effect of Portable Banking

Versatile banking significantly affects the monetary area:

Diminished Reliance on Actual Branches: Versatile banking has decreased the requirement for clients to visit actual bank offices for routine exchanges, saving time and assets for the two clients and monetary foundations.

Computerized Change: Conventional banks have needed to adjust to the advanced age, putting resources into portable financial framework and working on their internet based administrations to stay serious.

Fintech Incorporation: Portable financial stages frequently coordinate with fintech administrations, permitting clients to contribute, acquire individual credits, and access different monetary administration devices inside the equivalent application.

Monetary Consideration: Portable banking can possibly reach underserved populaces, furnishing them with banking access and administrations they probably won't have had in any case.

Remote Record Opening: A versatile banking applications offer the capacity to open new records from a distance, which can be particularly interesting to clients looking for a consistent onboarding experience.

Advantages of Portable Banking

Portable financial offers a scope of advantages to the two clients and monetary foundations:

Comfort: The capacity to perform monetary exchanges and oversee accounts whenever and anyplace is a huge accommodation for clients.

Cost Decrease: For banks, portable banking can diminish functional expenses related with actual branches, including framework and faculty costs.

Productivity: Portable banking smoothes out financial cycles, making exchanges quicker and more effective for clients.

Availability: Portable financial offers admittance to monetary administrations for people in regions with restricted actual branch inclusion.

Upgraded Security: Portable banking applications frequently highlight progressed safety efforts that safeguard client information and monetary exchanges.

Difficulties and Concerns

Notwithstanding its various benefits, portable banking likewise presents difficulties and concerns:

Security Dangers: The computerized idea of portable financial opens clients to different security dangers, including malware, phishing, and information breaks. Banks should ceaselessly put resources into safety efforts to safeguard their clients.

Advanced Education: Not all clients have a similar degree of computerized proficiency, which can make differences in their capacity to utilize versatile financial administrations successfully.

Client care: The change to advanced channels lessens eye to eye cooperations with bank staff, possibly influencing client connections and backing.

Security Concerns: Portable banking expects clients to share individual and monetary data internet, raising worries about information security and assurance.

Free time and Specialized Issues: Portable banking applications might encounter specialized misfires, prompting margin time that can baffle clients.

Computerized Gap: Not every person has equivalent admittance to the web and cell phones, making a computerized partition that can restrict monetary incorporation.

The Eventual fate of Versatile Banking

The fate of versatile banking is probably going to be molded by a few key patterns:

Trend setting innovation: Portable banking applications will keep on utilizing arising advancements like man-made reasoning and AI to offer customized types of assistance, improved security, and prescient bits of knowledge.

More extensive Combination: Portable banking applications will additionally coordinate with different monetary administrations, including cryptographic money, robo-guides, and computerized wallets, offering clients an exhaustive monetary environment.

Administrative Changes: Progressing administrative improvements will shape the scene of portable banking, zeroing in on information security, monetary security, and purchaser assurance.

Blockchain and Digital currencies: The reconciliation of blockchain innovation and the utilization of cryptographic forms of money might turn out to be more typical in versatile banking, offering improved security and effectiveness.

Monetary Incorporation: Endeavors to connect the computerized gap will keep, guaranteeing that versatile financial administrations are open to a more extensive populace.

Chapter 3

FinTech Disruption

Monetary innovation, or fintech, is reforming the monetary administrations industry by testing customary financial models, offering creative arrangements, and having an impact on the manner in which we cooperate with cash. The ascent of fintech has been fast, changing the way that we contribute, acquire, save, and make installments. This article investigates the troublesome powers and groundbreaking effect of fintech on monetary administrations.

The Fintech Scene

Fintech includes a great many monetary administrations and innovations, from installment handling and computerized wallets to robo-guides and shared loaning stages. It expects to upgrade monetary administrations by utilizing innovation and information to make them more available, effective, and client driven.

Key areas inside the fintech business include:

Installments and Moves: Fintech has improved and sped up the method involved with making installments and moving assets. Portable installment applications, advanced wallets, and blockchain-based arrangements empower people and organizations to send and get cash safely and rapidly.

Loaning and Acquiring: Shared loaning stages, online banks, and computerized credit suppliers offer elective getting choices to buyers and organizations, frequently with smoothed out application processes and quicker endorsement times.

Abundance The executives: Robo-consultants and online speculation stages use calculations to give mechanized, minimal expense, and customized venture counsel and portfolio the board administrations.

Insurtech: Insurtech organizations influence information investigation and computerized stages to improve the insurance business by offering more precise endorsing, quicker guarantees handling, and customized contracts.

Computerized Banking: Fintech new companies and advanced banks furnish banking administrations with no actual branches, offering serious charges, instinctive versatile applications, and highlights, for example, planning devices and no-expense ATM access.

Regtech: Administrative innovation, or regtech, assists monetary establishments with smoothing out consistence processes by utilizing information investigation, man-made consciousness, and mechanization.

Blockchain and Cryptographic forms of money: Blockchain innovation, which underlies digital currencies like Bitcoin, is upsetting monetary administrations by empowering straightforward, secure, and decentralized exchanges and making another resource class.

Interruption of Customary Banking

The fintech business' problematic impact is most apparent in its test to customary banking. Fintech organizations offer buyers and organizations elective arrangements that frequently beat the laid out financial models with regards to comfort, cost, and openness.

Further developed Client Experience: Fintech firms focus on client experience, frequently giving easy to use interfaces, nonstop access, and customized administrations. This differentiations with customary banks' inheritance frameworks and physical branches.

Lower Expenses: Online banks and fintech stages can offer lower charges and serious loan fees, as their more slender working models and robotized processes decrease above costs.

Improved Admittance: Fintech arrangements open up monetary administrations to a more extensive segment, including the people who are underbanked or unbanked. Versatile wallets and computerized financial administrations empower monetary consideration by permitting clients to get to banking administrations utilizing just a cell phone.

Imaginative Items: Fintech firms constantly enhance by growing new items and administrations, for example, miniature money management applications, robo-counsels, and advanced loaning stages, which meet the developing necessities of shoppers.

Speed and Effectiveness: Fintech organizations frequently succeed regarding velocity and productivity. For example, advance endorsement and dispensing cycles can require minutes rather than days, and installments can be made promptly, diminishing exchange times.

Open Banking: Open financial drives are changing the monetary scene by empowering the sharing of monetary information across foundations safely. This empowers shoppers to get to a more extensive scope of monetary administrations through a solitary stage or application.

Challenges and Administrative Contemplations

While fintech offers various advantages and inventive arrangements, it likewise presents difficulties and administrative contemplations that should be addressed to guarantee a steady and secure monetary biological system.

Administrative Consistence: Fintech firms should explore complex administrative systems, which can shift from one country to another. Consistence with information security, purchaser insurance, and hostile to illegal tax avoidance guidelines is critical.

Information Security: The fintech business relies upon tremendous measures of individual and monetary information, making it an objective for cyberattacks. Hearty safety efforts are fundamental to safeguard delicate data.

Buyer Insurance: As fintech grows, customer security issues should be tended to, including misrepresentation avoidance, debate goal, and information protection. Controllers need to find some kind of harmony between encouraging advancement and protecting purchasers.

Monetary Dependability: The fast development and advancing nature of fintech can present dangers to monetary security, especially on account of enormous scope reception of digital forms of money or blockchain-based frameworks.

Interoperability: Guaranteeing that different fintech arrangements can cooperate effectively is fundamental for the monetary environment's general usefulness. Normalization and cooperation are key variables in accomplishing interoperability.

Blockchain and Digital forms of money

Blockchain innovation and digital forms of money address one of the main interruptions inside fintech. This is the way they are changing the monetary scene:

Straightforwardness and Security: Blockchain innovation gives an unchanging and straightforward record, upgrading security and decreasing misrepresentation in monetary exchanges. It is being embraced in different applications, for example, production network the executives, for its recognizability highlights.

Cross-Line Exchanges: Digital currencies, like Bitcoin and Wave, offer an option in contrast to conventional cross-line installment frameworks. They give a quicker, more financially savvy answer for global cash moves.

Decentralization: The decentralized idea of blockchain innovation challenges conventional monetary go-betweens. Decentralized finance (DeFi) stages use blockchain to empower shared loaning, decentralized trades, and yield cultivating.

Tokenization of Resources: Blockchain empowers the fragmentary proprietorship and move of certifiable resources, like land, craftsmanship, and stocks, through tokenization. This could make effective financial planning more open to a more extensive scope of people.

Brilliant Agreements: Savvy contracts on blockchain stages, like Ethereum, empower robotized and trustless execution of agreements, possibly supplanting go-betweens in different legitimate and monetary arrangements.

The Eventual fate of Fintech Interruption

The fintech unrest makes it clear that things are not pulling back. Key patterns and improvements to look for before long include:

Proceeded with Advancement: Fintech will keep on developing, presenting new items and administrations that upgrade monetary availability, productivity, and client experience.

Expanded Joint effort: Fintech firms might work together more with customary monetary organizations, making a mix of imaginative innovation and laid out monetary skill.

Blockchain Incorporation: Blockchain innovation and cryptographic forms of money will keep on impacting fintech and monetary administrations, with national banks investigating the capability of national bank advanced monetary forms (CBDCs).

Worldwide Extension: Fintech organizations will grow their range universally, possibly making monetary administrations more open and reasonable in developing business sectors.

Monetary Consideration: Fintech will assume a significant part in working on monetary consideration, permitting underserved and unbanked populaces to get to fundamental monetary administrations.

3.1Rise of FinTech Startups

Throughout the last 10 years, FinTech (Monetary Innovation) new businesses have picked up huge speed and disturbed the customary monetary administrations industry. These imaginative organizations influence innovation to give current, client driven monetary arrangements, having an impact on the manner in which we deal with our cash, contribute, make installments, and connect with monetary establishments. This article investigates the ascent of FinTech new businesses and their effect on the money area.

The Introduction of FinTech

The expression "FinTech" is a portmanteau of "monetary" and "innovation," and it alludes to the utilization of innovation to convey monetary administrations in a more effective and imaginative way. The FinTech development built up some decent momentum directly following the 2008 monetary emergency when there was a developing interest for elective monetary administrations and expanded doubt in customary financial establishments.

Key Drivers of the FinTech Blast

A few variables have added to the quick ascent of FinTech new companies:

Mechanical Headways: The progression of advanced innovation, cell phones, and the web has made it simpler to get to and oversee monetary administrations internet, preparing for FinTech development.

Buyer Interest: Customers progressively look for more advantageous, practical, and easy to understand monetary administrations. FinTech new companies answer this interest with simple to-utilize applications and stages.

Administrative Changes: Administrative changes, like open financial drives and steady administrative systems, have given open doors to FinTech organizations to get to information and contend in the monetary business.

Lower Hindrances to Passage: The accessibility of distributed computing, open-source programming, and APIs (Application Programming Points of interaction) has brought the boundaries down to section for new businesses, empowering them to quickly create and scale their administrations more.

Financial backer Premium: Financial backers are emptying capital into FinTech new companies, perceiving their capability to upset and develop monetary administrations.

Different FinTech Contributions

FinTech new companies length a large number of monetary administrations, including:

Computerized Banking: Advanced banks or neobanks offer online-just financial administrations, frequently with no actual branches. These banks give simple record arrangement, lower expenses, and easy to understand versatile applications for overseeing funds.

Installment and Cash Move: FinTech organizations have upset the manner in which we make installments and move cash. Portable installment applications and computerized wallets have acquired notoriety, while cross-line cash move administrations have made worldwide exchanges quicker and more financially savvy.

Shared Loaning: P2P loaning stages interface borrowers with individual or institutional moneylenders, offering cutthroat financing costs and a smoothed out application process.

Robo-Guides: Robo-counsels use calculations to give mechanized speculation exhortation and portfolio the board administrations. They offer enhanced venture choices with lower the executives expenses than customary monetary counselors.

InsurTech: Protection innovation (InsurTech) new companies utilize information examination and computerized stages to smooth out the protection interaction, from endorsing to claims the executives.

RegTech: Administrative innovation (RegTech) organizations help monetary establishments in overseeing and conforming to complex administrative prerequisites by utilizing information examination and robotization.

Blockchain and Cryptographic forms of money: New businesses in the blockchain and digital money space offer decentralized and secure monetary administrations, including advanced resource exchanging, decentralized finance (DeFi), and starting coin contributions (ICOs).

Influence on Conventional Banking

The ascent of FinTech new companies significantly affects conventional financial foundations. While laid out banks have needed to adjust and enhance to stay cutthroat, they additionally face difficulties as they explore the developing monetary scene:

Improved Client Experience: FinTech organizations focus on client experience, offering more easy to understand interfaces and quicker, more advantageous administrations. Customary banks are feeling the squeeze to further develop their client support and computerized contributions.

Contest and Joint effort: A few customary banks have decided to team up with FinTech new companies to use their innovation and arrive at new business sectors. In any case, this has likewise prompted expanded rivalry as FinTech organizations infringe an on customary financial area.

Diminished Working Expenses: FinTech new businesses frequently work with more slender designs, utilizing mechanization and innovation to decrease functional expenses. This cost advantage constrains customary banks to smooth out their activities and cut costs.

Advancement and Item Improvement: FinTech firms are known for their dexterity and development. They habitually send off new items and administrations to meet the developing necessities of customers, inciting conventional banks to embrace a more creative mentality.

Monetary Incorporation: FinTech new businesses are growing admittance to monetary administrations, especially for underserved or unbanked populaces. Customary banks are likewise investigating ways of working on monetary consideration by digitizing their administrations.

Difficulties and Dangers

Notwithstanding their many benefits, FinTech new businesses additionally face difficulties and dangers, including:

Administrative Consistence: Exploring complex and developing monetary guidelines can be difficult for FinTech organizations. Consistence with information assurance, buyer insurance, and against illegal tax avoidance regulations is critical.

Network safety Worries: As monetary innovation organizations handle tremendous measures of delicate monetary and individual information, they are practical objectives for cyberattacks. Strong network safety measures are fundamental to safeguard against information breaks.

Market Immersion: The FinTech business is turning out to be progressively packed, making it more trying for new companies to stick out and acquire portion of the overall industry.

Financing and Maintainability: Some FinTech new companies face difficulties in getting reasonable subsidizing as they work to lay out their organizations. The business' fast development and changing financial backer feeling can influence subsidizing open doors.

The Fate of FinTech New businesses

The fate of FinTech new companies looks splendid, with a few patterns and improvements to watch:

Proceeded with Development: FinTech new companies will keep on presenting new, imaginative items and administrations, further changing the monetary administrations scene.

Worldwide Development: FinTech organizations will grow their scope, both locally and globally, utilizing computerized stages to offer monetary administrations to a more extensive scope of clients.

Blockchain and Cryptographic forms of money: As blockchain and digital currencies mature, they will assume an undeniably critical part in monetary administrations, offering decentralized, secure, and effective arrangements.

More prominent Monetary Incorporation: FinTech new companies will keep on driving monetary consideration, furnishing underserved and unbanked populaces with admittance to fundamental monetary administrations.

3.2Peer-to-Peer Lending and Crowdfunding

Shared (P2P) loaning has arisen as a momentous technique for borrowers to get credits by interfacing straightforwardly with individual financial backers or moneylenders. P2P loaning stages go about as mediators, working with this immediate association and bypassing customary financial establishments. This approach democratizes loaning and has critical ramifications for borrowers and financial backers the same.

Availability and Inclusivity: P2P loaning stages make getting to credit more comprehensive and open. Borrowers range from people looking for individual advances to private ventures needing working capital. This inclusivity has changed the loaning scene, offering open doors for those with credit imperatives or restricted insurance.

Proficient Application Cycles: P2P loaning works on the acquiring experience with smoothed out application processes and frequently quicker endorsement times contrasted with conventional banks. This easy to use approach takes special care of an expansive range of borrowers, encouraging a more proficient loaning climate.

High level Credit Appraisal: P2P loaning stages utilize complex calculations and credit scoring models to evaluate borrower financial soundness. These frameworks coordinate borrowers with reasonable moneylenders in light of their gamble resistance and speculation targets, improving the proficiency and adequacy of loaning.

Enhancement and Better yields: Financial backers in P2P loaning stages have the valuable chance to differentiate their portfolios by choosing credits that line up with their gamble profiles. This enhancement can prompt better yields contrasted with conventional bank accounts or fixed-pay speculations.

Auxiliary Business sectors: Some P2P stages offer optional business sectors where financial backers can trade credits, expanding the liquidity and adaptability of their speculations. These optional business sectors add an additional layer of development and opportunity to P2P loaning.

Crowdfunding: Empowering Aggregate Gathering pledges

Crowdfunding is an aggregate gathering pledges model that permits people and organizations to raise assets from an enormous pool of benefactors through internet based stages. This flexible methodology has applications across different areas, giving open doors to makers, business visionaries, and donors to get to capital and backing causes they are energetic about.

Various Applications: Crowdfunding isn't restricted to a particular industry. It has been utilized to subsidize a large number of ventures, from inventive undertakings and worthy missions to startup dispatches and land improvements. Its flexibility makes it a significant device for a wide range of adventures.

Financial backer Cooperation: Crowdfunding democratizes raising money by permitting ordinary people to become financial backers. This participatory component is alluring to the people who need to help ventures and organizations they have confidence in, producing a more special interaction among benefactors and the causes they support.

Administrative Structures: Various sorts of crowdfunding, including value crowdfunding, gift based crowdfunding, and reward-based crowdfunding, might be dependent upon different administrative systems relying upon the area. These administrative changes plan to legitimize and safeguard the two financial backers and business people partaking in crowdfunding exercises.

Impetuses for Sponsor: Crowdfunding efforts regularly offer motivations to benefactors, for example, early admittance to items, value offers, or restrictive prizes. These motivations make the crowdfunding experience connecting with and commonly advantageous for the two makers and allies.

Local area Building: Crowdfunding makes a feeling of local area around projects, as patrons feel a special interaction to the causes they support. This people group driven approach can encourage more grounded commitment and backing for different endeavors.

3.3Blockchain and Cryptocurrencies

Blockchain innovation and cryptographic forms of money have arisen as two of the most extraordinary and problematic advancements of the 21st hundred years, testing conventional monetary frameworks, reshaping different ventures, and reclassifying the manner in which we contemplate exchanges, information security, and confidence in the computerized age. In this article, we investigate the hidden ideas, the effect, and the likely future of blockchain and digital currencies.

Blockchain Innovation: The Computerized Record Upheaval

At its center, blockchain is a decentralized and dispersed computerized record used to record exchanges across an organization of PCs. In contrast to customary concentrated frameworks, blockchain disposes of the requirement for mediators, like banks or states, to confirm and manage exchanges. A portion of the critical highlights of blockchain innovation include:

Decentralization: Blockchain works on a shared organization, with duplicates of the record put away on different PCs, known as hubs. This decentralization guarantees that no single substance has unlimited authority over the organization, improving security and straightforwardness.

Straightforwardness: Exchanges recorded on the blockchain are noticeable to all members in the organization. This straightforwardness cultivates trust and responsibility, as all gatherings can freely check the exchange history.

Security: Blockchain utilizes cryptographic methods and agreement systems to get the organization, making it profoundly impervious to unapproved access or altering. Exchanges are kept in "blocks," making a changeless record.

Brilliant Agreements: Shrewd agreements are self-executing concurrences with predefined rules and conditions. They robotize contract execution when explicit circumstances are met, wiping out the requirement for go-betweens.

Permissioned versus Permissionless Blockchains: Blockchain organizations can be either permissioned or permissionless. Permissioned blockchains expect members to acquire endorsement to join the organization, while permissionless blockchains, as Bitcoin and Ethereum, permit anybody to take an interest.

Cryptographic forms of money: The Computerized Cash Unrest

Cryptographic forms of money are computerized or virtual monetary standards that utilization cryptographic procedures for security. They are one of the most unmistakable utilizations of blockchain innovation, giving a decentralized and computerized option in contrast to customary monetary standards. Key attributes of cryptographic forms of money include:

Decentralization: Cryptographic forms of money are not constrained by national banks or legislatures. They work autonomously, empowering monetary exchanges that are liberated from legislative impact or impedance.

Worldwide Availability: Digital currencies are open to anybody with a web association, making them comprehensive for people all over the planet, particularly those without admittance to conventional financial administrations.

Secrecy: Numerous digital currencies offer a degree of protection, permitting clients to make exchanges without uncovering their true characters. While this component can upgrade security, it has likewise raised worries about possible abuse.

Restricted Supply: A few digital forms of money, like Bitcoin, have a covered stockpile, significance there is a most extreme number of coins that can at any point be made. This shortage is much of the time refered to as an element adding to their possible worth.

Unpredictability: Digital currencies are known at their cost unpredictability, encountering huge changes in esteem over brief periods. This instability has made them alluring to financial backers looking for exceptional yields however has likewise raised worries about their dependability.

Influence on Money: A Troublesome Power

Blockchain innovation and cryptographic forms of money considerably affect the monetary business, changing customary banking and installment frameworks. Here are a portion of the critical manners by which they have impacted finance:

Computerized Installments: Digital currencies offer an option in contrast to customary installment strategies, considering quick and financially savvy cross-line exchanges. They decrease the requirement for delegate banks and money trade administrations.

Monetary Consideration: Digital forms of money can possibly offer monetary types of assistance to unbanked and underbanked populaces, permitting individuals without admittance to conventional financial frameworks to store, move, and get reserves.

Brilliant Agreements: Savvy contracts robotize the execution of monetary arrangements, lessening the requirement for middle people like banks, legal advisors, and escrow administrations. This can prompt quicker and less expensive agreement execution.

Beginning Coin Contributions (ICOs): ICOs are gathering pledges components that empower new companies and undertakings to raise capital by giving tokens on a blockchain. While they offer new open doors for gathering pledges, they have additionally raised worries about extortion and administrative consistence.

Decentralized Money (DeFi): DeFi is an arising biological system of monetary applications based on blockchain stages. It incorporates loaning, getting, exchanging, and yield cultivating, all working without customary delegates. DeFi has developed quickly, drawing in the two clients and financial backers, however it additionally faces administrative difficulties.

National Bank Computerized Monetary forms (CBDCs): A few national banks are investigating the improvement of computerized variants of their public monetary forms. These CBDCs mean to consolidate the upsides of cryptographic forms of money, like quick and effective exchanges, with the security and administrative oversight of conventional monetary standards.

Difficulties and Concerns: The Way ahead

Notwithstanding their true capacity, blockchain and digital currencies face a few difficulties and worries that should be tended to for far and wide reception and steadiness:

Administrative Vulnerability: The administrative climate for digital currencies is as yet developing. State run administrations and monetary controllers overall are attempting to lay out clear rules and rules, influencing the reception and utilization of digital forms of money.

Unpredictability: Digital currencies are known at their cost instability, introducing speculation amazing open doors as well as dangers. Huge value changes can happen over brief periods, prompting worries about security.

Security Dangers: While blockchain innovation is for the most part viewed as secure, weaknesses and hacking episodes have happened. Clients should play it safe to safeguard their resources and information.

Security and Secrecy: The namelessness elements of some digital currencies have raised worries about their expected use for criminal operations, for example, illegal tax avoidance and tax avoidance. Administrative specialists are progressively centered around resolving these issues.

Versatility: Blockchain networks face versatility challenges, especially in dealing with a high volume of exchanges. Settling versatility issues is essential for blockchain innovation to help a more extensive scope of utilizations.

Natural Effect: The energy utilization of certain blockchain networks, especially those utilizing evidence of-work agreement systems, has raised worries about their ecological effect.

The Eventual fate of Blockchain and Cryptographic forms of money

The future of blockchain and cryptographic forms of money holds huge commitment and vulnerability. The innovation's potential applications stretch out a long ways past money, enveloping store network the board, medical care, casting a ballot frameworks, and that's just the beginning. As states, organizations, and clients keep on investigating the potential outcomes and address difficulties, blockchain and cryptographic forms of money will probably assume a filling part in molding the computerized scene.

Blockchain innovation will proceed to advance and track down its direction into different areas, offering improved security, straightforwardness, and effectiveness. Cryptographic forms of money, then again, may additionally incorporate with conventional monetary frameworks or keep on advancing as discrete computerized resources. Whether for of installment, a venture vehicle, or a device for robotizing gets, the effect of blockchain and digital currencies on the worldwide economy will be a subject of progressing conversation, guideline, and development in the years to come. The way ahead includes finding some kind of harmony between encouraging development and guaranteeing administrative consistence and shopper insurance.

3.4Impact on Traditional Banking

Conventional financial foundations have been encountering critical interruption because of the development of blockchain innovation and cryptographic forms of money.

These advancements can possibly reshape the monetary scene, testing laid out financial models and offering the two valuable open doors and difficulties. In this article, we will investigate the effect of blockchain and digital currencies on conventional banking.

1. **Disintermediation: Decreasing the Requirement for Middle people**

   Blockchain innovation, through its decentralized and trustless nature, can possibly essentially diminish the requirement for middle people in monetary exchanges. In conventional banking, middle people like banks and installment processors assume a focal part in working with exchanges, forcing expenses and defers on clients. With blockchain, distributed exchanges can happen straightforwardly between parties, removing agents.

For instance, digital currencies like Bitcoin empower clients to send reserves straightforwardly to each other, killing the requirement for banks as mediators in cross-line exchanges. This disintermediation can prompt quicker and more practical exchanges, at last testing the customary financial charge structure.

2. **Cross-Line Exchanges: Altering Worldwide Installments**

   One of the most recognizable effects of blockchain and digital currencies on conventional banking is their impact on cross-line exchanges. Customary worldwide cash moves can be slow, costly, and liable to swapping scale variances. Digital currencies, then again, offer an answer for these difficulties.

   Blockchain-based digital currencies work with almost moment cross-line exchanges for a portion of the expense contrasted with customary financial administrations. This can essentially help people, organizations, and even banks that decide to take on these advancements for global settlements. To remain serious, conventional banks are investigating ways of utilizing blockchain for worldwide exchanges and settlements.

3. **Improved Security and Straightforwardness: Building Trust**

   Blockchain's inborn security highlights make it alluring for use in monetary frameworks. Exchanges recorded on a blockchain are secure, straightforward, and changeless. Each member in the organization can autonomously check the exchange history, lessening the gamble of extortion or blunder.

   Conventional financial establishments have confronted difficulties connected with security breaks and information uprightness. The utilization of blockchain innovation can reinforce safety efforts, making it more challenging for unapproved gatherings to think twice about monetary information. This improved security and straightforwardness can construct trust among clients, diminishing the gamble of information breaks and extortion.

4. **Brilliant Agreements: Robotization of Monetary Arrangements**

   Savvy gets, a component of some blockchain stages, are self-executing concurrences with predefined rules and conditions. They mechanize contract execution when explicit circumstances are met, decreasing the requirement for delegates in different monetary cycles.

   For example, savvy agreements can work with mechanized credit distributions, installments, and even protection claims. Conventional banks are investigating the coordination of savvy agreements to smooth out their tasks and decrease above costs. This computerization can make monetary cycles more proficient and savvy.

5. **Advanced Banking and Development: Answering Client Assumptions**
   The ascent of cryptographic forms of money and the reception of blockchain innovation have pushed conventional banks to embrace computerized change and advancement. Clients progressively expect easy to use computerized financial administrations that offer accommodation and availability.
   To measure up to these assumptions, customary banks are putting resources into the improvement of easy to use portable applications, computerized wallets, and internet banking stages. They are likewise investigating new elements like planning devices and robo-counsels to stay cutthroat in a changing monetary scene.
6. **National Bank Computerized Monetary standards (CBDCs): A Changing Scene**

A few national banks overall are investigating the improvement of national bank computerized monetary standards (CBDCs). These computerized adaptations of public monetary standards expect to consolidate the advantages of digital forms of money, like quick and effective exchanges, with the steadiness and administrative oversight of customary monetary forms.

CBDCs could reshape the connection between conventional banks and national banks. They could affect how cash is conveyed, put away, and moved, with likely ramifications for money related arrangement, monetary dependability, and banking tasks.

Difficulties and Worries for Customary Banks

While blockchain and digital currencies offer various benefits and amazing open doors, they likewise present difficulties and worries for customary banks:

Administrative Consistence: The administrative climate for digital currencies is as yet advancing. Conventional banks should explore complex and developing administrative structures to guarantee consistence with hostile to tax evasion (AML) and know your client (KYC) guidelines.

Risk The board: The instability of digital currencies is a huge concern. Customary banks should cautiously evaluate the dangers related with offering digital money related benefits and safeguard themselves from expected misfortunes.

Security: While blockchain is viewed as secure, there have been occurrences of weaknesses and hacking. Banks should put resources into vigorous network safety measures to safeguard against potential information breaks or unapproved access.

Client Schooling: Numerous clients are not knowledgeable in blockchain and digital currency innovation. Banks should instruct their clients and proposition direction on capable and secure use.

Contest from Fintech and Neobanks: Conventional banks face rivalry from cryptographic forms of money as well as from fintech new businesses and advanced banks. To stay significant, they should enhance and offer easy to use advanced administrations.

The Fate of Conventional Banking

The effect of blockchain and cryptographic forms of money on customary banking is irrefutable, and it will keep on molding the business' future. Conventional banks should adjust to the changing scene by embracing advanced change, investigating blockchain innovation, and answering client assumptions for comfort and development.

Blockchain and digital forms of money are probably going to coincide with customary banking, offering a scope of monetary arrangements. Banks that decisively influence blockchain and digital forms of money can improve their tasks, cut costs, and convey better administrations to their clients.

As the administrative climate develops, conventional banks might track down better approaches to coordinate these developments into their contributions and stay cutthroat in a quickly developing monetary biological system.

Chapter 4

Banking And Big Data

The crossing point of banking and enormous information has prompted a change in outlook in the monetary business. With monstrous volumes of information produced consistently, banks are saddling the force of large information to pursue more educated choices, further develop client encounters, upgrade risk the board, and smooth out tasks. In this article, we investigate how large information is reshaping the financial area, its key applications, challenges, and the fate of information driven finance.

Seeing Huge Information in Banking

Large information alludes to the huge and complex datasets that are past the abilities of customary information handling instruments. It incorporates huge volumes of data as well as information assortment (organized and unstructured), speed (speed of information age), and veracity (information precision and quality). The usage of huge information in banking includes gathering, handling, and dissecting this abundance of data to determine important bits of knowledge and backing direction.

Key Utilizations of Huge Information in Banking

Risk The board:

Credit Scoring: Customary credit scoring models frequently depend on a restricted arrangement of data of interest, like record and pay. Large information empowers banks to think about a more extensive scope of variables, including virtual entertainment movement, online way of behaving, and exchange chronicles, to precisely survey a candidate's financial soundness more.

Extortion Location: Large information examination can distinguish fake exercises by dissecting exchange designs and recognizing abnormalities. Banks use AI calculations to screen exchanges continuously, hailing dubious way of behaving and limiting monetary misfortunes because of misrepresentation.

Market and Financial Examination: Enormous information devices can investigate tremendous measures of data from different sources to give bits of knowledge into market patterns, monetary circumstances, and international occasions. This investigation assists manages an account with pursuing better venture and loaning choices.

Client Bits of knowledge and Personalization:

Division and Focusing on: Banks utilize enormous information to portion their client base all the more successfully. By grasping client conduct, inclinations, and socioeconomics, they can tailor items, administrations, and showcasing efforts to explicit client fragments.

Proposal Frameworks: Customized suggestions, driven by large information calculations, empower banks to recommend items and administrations that are pertinent to individual clients. This further develops client commitment and drives strategically pitching valuable open doors.

Functional Productivity:

Prescient Support: Banks utilize huge information investigation to screen and keep up with their IT foundation and actual resources. By anticipating when hardware might fall flat or require support, they can diminish personal time and lower functional expenses.

Process Improvement: Enormous information is utilized to investigate and upgrade different inward cycles, for example, credit beginning, client onboarding, and misrepresentation avoidance. Process improvement can prompt expense investment funds and better client encounters.

Administrative Consistence:

Against Tax evasion (AML): Large information advancements assist manages an account with distinguishing dubious exchanges and consent to AML guidelines. Overwhelmingly of exchange information, they can recognize designs characteristic of illegal tax avoidance or other unlawful exercises.

Know Your Client (KYC): Banks can utilize large information to smooth out the KYC cycle by collecting information from different sources to check client personalities and evaluate the gamble level related with every client.

Challenges in Carrying out Large Information in Banking

While large information offers huge advantages for the financial business, it additionally presents difficulties:

Information Protection and Security: Taking care of touchy monetary information accompanies an increased liability regarding defending client data. Banks should put vigorously in information security and follow information assurance guidelines.

Information Quality: The precision and dependability of information are vital. Mistaken or deficient information can prompt incorrect bits of knowledge and direction. Banks need to lay out information administration practices to guarantee information quality.

Information Combination: Banks frequently have heritage frameworks with information put away in storehouses. Coordinating information from these divergent frameworks can be complicated however is fundamental for a bound together perspective on client data.

Ability and Mastery: The interest for information researchers and investigators is high. Banks need to draw in and hold ability with the important abilities to actually oversee and break down enormous information.

Administrative Consistence: Banks should explore complex administrative scenes. Consenting to information security, hostile to illegal tax avoidance, and purchaser protection regulations is significant.

Adaptability: As information volumes keep on developing, banks should put resources into versatile framework to deal with the expanded information load.

The Eventual fate of Large Information in Banking

The fate of large information in banking is promising, with a few energizing improvements not too far off:

AI and artificial intelligence Progressions: AI and computerized reasoning will keep on assuming a focal part in large information examination. These advancements will turn out to be more refined, empowering banks to go with additional precise forecasts and computerize choice making processes.

Ongoing Information Examination: The capacity to dissect information progressively will turn out to be more basic. Banks will utilize continuous investigation for extortion discovery, client service, and market examination.

Improved Client Experience: Banks will progressively zero in on conveying customized and frictionless client encounters. Large information will empower them to expect client needs, offer custom fitted arrangements, and offer consistent computerized types of assistance.

Blockchain Mix: Blockchain innovation, with its protected and straightforward record, will track down additional applications in banking. It can work on cross-line installments, further develop recognizability of exchanges, and upgrade trust in monetary frameworks.

Quantum Figuring: The appearance of quantum registering will significantly affect enormous information examination. It will empower banks to process and investigate tremendous datasets at speeds presently impossible.

Open Banking: Open financial drives and guidelines will work with information dividing among banks and outsider suppliers. Huge information examination will be instrumental in utilizing this common information to offer new and imaginative monetary administrations.

4.1Data Analytics in Banking

Information examination has reformed the financial business, reshaping the manner in which monetary foundations work, serve their clients, and settle on basic choices. In a period characterized by computerized change and information driven direction, information examination has arisen as a urgent device that engages banks to improve risk the executives, client care, extortion identification, functional proficiency, and the sky is the limit from there. This article dives into the meaning of information examination in banking, its complex applications, and the significant effect it has on the area.

The Development of Information Examination in Banking

Lately, information examination has seen dramatic development in the financial area, to a great extent driven overwhelmingly of information produced, gathered, and put away by monetary organizations. The use of information examination has developed from fundamental announcing and elucidating investigation to further developed prescient and prescriptive examination.

This advancement has empowered banks to infer important bits of knowledge and drive vital choices, at last working on their general execution.

Risk The board and Information Examination

One of the essential uses of information examination in banking is risk the board. Banks are presented to different kinds of dangers, including credit risk, market risk, and functional gamble. To really deal with these dangers, banks depend on information investigation to evaluate and moderate likely dangers.

Credit Hazard The executives: Information examination assumes a vital part in credit risk evaluation. Conventional strategies for assessing a borrower's reliability have been supplemented, and at times, supplanted by information driven models. These models utilize verifiable information to decide the probability of a borrower defaulting on a credit. Factors like record of loan repayment, pay, business status, and existing obligation are viewed as in credit scoring models, assisting keeps money with pursuing more educated loaning choices and lessen the gamble of defaults.

Market Chance Examination: Monetary business sectors are profoundly unique, and banks need to remain cautious to alleviate market risk. Information investigation empowers banks to follow market patterns, dissect authentic market information, and model different situations to more readily figure out expected chances. By distinguishing market variances and surveying their expected effect, banks can make convenient changes in accordance with their portfolios and venture methodologies.

Functional Gamble Moderation: Functional dangers originate from inside cycles and frameworks, and information examination can help banks recognize and relieve these dangers. By examining functional information, banks can pinpoint bottlenecks, shortcomings, and areas of likely disappointment. This, thus, considers process improvement, asset distribution, and a decrease in functional expenses.

Improving Client care with Information Investigation

Banks approach an abundance of information about their clients, going from exchange narratives to site conduct. Information examination changes this crude information into significant bits of knowledge that can be utilized to improve client care and convey a predominant client experience.

Customized Client Commitment: By breaking down client information, banks can acquire a profound comprehension of client conduct, inclinations, and requirements. Equipped with this information, banks can make exceptionally customized offers, advancements, and item proposals. This degree of personalization fortifies client connections as well as drives strategically pitching and upselling open doors.

Chatbots and Menial helpers: Client assistance has additionally been reformed by information examination. Chatbots and menial helpers, controlled by regular language handling and AI, are being conveyed by banks to offer nonstop help. These computer based intelligence driven devices can comprehend and answer client requests, address routine worries, and proposition moment arrangements, guaranteeing a consistent and productive client care insight.

Extortion Identification and Avoidance

The financial business is an ideal objective for fraudsters and cybercriminals. Information examination plays had a basic impact in recognizing and forestalling false exercises, eventually protecting the interests of banks and their clients.

Constant Extortion Recognition: Customary rule-based frameworks are as of now not adequate to battle progressively refined misrepresentation endeavors. Information examination arrangements are intended to distinguish unusual examples and irregularities in exchanges. By consistently observing exchange information and contrasting it with authentic examples, banks can rapidly recognize possibly deceitful exercises progressively.

Conduct Examination: Social investigation is an integral asset that banks use to identify extortion. By examining the way of behaving of clients over the long haul, banks can recognize uncommon examples or deviations from laid out standards. For instance, in the event that a client ordinarily makes exchanges inside a specific geological region yet unexpectedly begins making exchanges from an alternate area, this adjustment of conduct might set off a caution for additional examination.

Functional Effectiveness and Information Investigation

Functional effectiveness is a vital target for banks, and information examination assumes a huge part in accomplishing this objective. Banks work with different manual and tedious cycles, which can be smoothed out and streamlined through information investigation.

Process Mechanization: Information investigation empowers banks to robotize numerous manual and dreary assignments, decreasing the potential for human blunder and saving important time and assets. Undertakings like information passage, report age, and consistence checks can be computerized, opening up workers to zero in on higher-esteem exercises.

Work process Enhancement: By investigating functional work processes, information examination recognizes bottlenecks, failures, and regions that require improvement. This information driven approach permits banks to enhance processes, distribute assets all the more successfully, and lessen functional expenses.

Utilizing Enormous Information for Prescient Investigation

The time of large information has changed the potential outcomes of information examination in banking. Banks are presently managing enormous volumes of organized and unstructured information from different sources, including web-based entertainment, outer market information, and client communications.

Prescient Investigation: Prescient examination use large information to expect future occasions and patterns. By investigating authentic information and joining it with outside information sources, banks can foresee client conduct, market patterns, and likely dangers. For instance, banks can utilize virtual entertainment information to measure client opinion and adjust their advertising procedures in like manner.

Information Driven Independent direction: Banks are progressively utilizing information investigation to help their essential dynamic cycles. Information driven experiences help in the improvement of new items and administrations, market development systems, and the streamlining of inward activities. This approach guarantees that choices depend on experimental proof instead of instinct.

Administrative Consistence and Information Investigation

Banks are dependent upon a huge number of monetary guidelines and consistence prerequisites. Information examination assumes a pivotal part in assisting saves money with meeting these commitments by observing and covering exchanges and exercises progressively.

Against Illegal tax avoidance (AML) and Know Your Client (KYC): AML and KYC guidelines expect banks to recognize and confirm their clients, as well as identify and report dubious exchanges. Information investigation assists keeps money with robotizing the most common way of distinguishing high-risk clients, observing exchanges for surprising examples, and creating reports for administrative specialists.

Basel III and Capital Sufficiency: Administrative capital prerequisites, as specified under Basel III, order that banks keep a specific degree of capital ampleness. Information investigation assists manages an account with surveying their capital sufficiency by demonstrating and breaking down their gamble openness, stress-testing their portfolios, and guaranteeing consistence with administrative capital necessities.

4.2Personalization and Customer Insights

In the present information driven world, personalization and client bits of knowledge have become key to the outcome of organizations across different ventures. Whether it's internet business, medical services, or diversion, understanding client inclinations and fitting encounters in like manner can be a distinct advantage. In this article, we'll dive into the significant effect of personalization and the job of client experiences in driving business development.

The Period of Personalization

Personalization is the act of conveying customized encounters, items, or administrations to individual clients in view of their inclinations, ways of behaving, and socioeconomics. It's anything but another idea, however it has acquired exceptional noticeable quality with the multiplication of computerized innovation and the immense measures of information accessible.

Web based business: In the realm of internet shopping, personalization has reformed the manner in which buyers cooperate with brands. Web based business stages dissect your perusing history, buy conduct, and socioeconomics to prescribe items you're probably going to be keen on. Amazon's suggestion motor is a great representation of this. Thusly, they further develop client experience as well as increment deals by showing clients items they're bound to buy.

Real time features: Organizations like Netflix and Spotify have excelled at personalization. They use calculations to examine what motion pictures, Programs, or music you've drawn in with and propose content suggestions that match your preferences.

This keeps you on their foundation longer as well as assists them with understanding your inclinations all the more profoundly, accordingly refining suggestions after some time.

Virtual Entertainment: Web-based entertainment stages use personalization to arrange your newsfeed and ads. They examine your commitment history, the substance you've loved or shared, and your associations with companions to show you a greater amount of what you need to see. This personalization keeps clients drew in and, according to a business point of view, helps promotion focusing on and income.

The Worth of Personalization

Further developed Client Experience: Personalization upgrades the client experience by making it more important and locking in. Clients appreciate when organizations grasp their necessities and inclinations. It can prompt expanded client dedication and fulfillment.

Higher Changes: Customized proposals and offers are bound to change over into deals. At the point when clients see items or administrations that line up with their inclinations, they are more disposed to make a buy.

Information Driven Direction: Personalization depends on gathering and investigating client information. This information can be priceless in understanding business sector patterns, client conduct, and regions for development.

Upgraded Client Maintenance: Customized encounters can assemble long haul client connections. At the point when clients feel that a brand comprehends and esteems them, they are bound to return for future buys.

Utilizing Client Experiences

Personalization wouldn't be imaginable without a profound comprehension of client conduct and inclinations. This understanding is acquired through client experiences, which are the consequences of information examination and statistical surveying. Here are a few critical parts of utilizing client experiences:

Information Assortment: The underpinning of client bits of knowledge is information. This information can be gathered from different sources, including client communications, overviews, site investigation, web-based entertainment, and buy accounts. The more information you have, the more complete your experiences will be.

Information Investigation: When you have information, the subsequent stage is to break down it. Information investigation can uncover examples, patterns, and connections that give significant bits of knowledge into client conduct. This cycle frequently requires the utilization of information investigation devices and advancements.

Division: Not all clients are something similar. Division is the act of separating your client base into more modest gatherings in view of shared qualities or ways of behaving. This takes into consideration more designated advertising and personalization endeavors.

Criticism Systems: Effectively looking for input from clients is fundamental. Overviews, audits, and direct correspondence channels can give important data that goes past what crude information can uncover.

Statistical surveying: Past client information, statistical surveying can give bits of knowledge into industry patterns, contenders, and market elements. It's fundamental to comprehend the more extensive setting where your business works.

Uses of Client Bits of knowledge

Item Advancement: Client bits of knowledge can direct item improvement by assisting organizations with understanding what clients need and need. It can illuminate choices about item elements, plan, and valuing.

Showcasing and Promoting: Client experiences are priceless in creating advertising efforts and ads. They assist you with fitting your informing to the particular inclinations and trouble spots of your main interest group.

Client care: Client bits of knowledge can be utilized to further develop client care by distinguishing normal issues or concerns. It additionally empowers the improvement of self-administration instruments and assets that address normal client questions.

Estimating Techniques: Understanding client conduct and eagerness to pay is vital in setting cutthroat and productive valuing systems. Client experiences can uncover how cost delicate your client base is.

Challenges and Moral Contemplations

While personalization and client bits of knowledge offer significant advantages, there are additionally moves and moral contemplations to explore.

Information Protection: With the assortment of tremendous measures of client information, organizations should focus on information protection and security. Clients should be educated about how their information is utilized and have the choice to quit.

Predisposition: Client information can here and there contain inclinations, which can prompt uncalled for or erroneous personalization. For instance, assuming an online business stage just prescribes top of the line items to specific socioeconomics, it propagates inclination and cutoff points valuable open doors for other client portions.

Overpersonalization: There is a scarcely discernible difference between compelling personalization and crawling clients out with excessively nitty gritty suggestions. It is critical to Work out some kind of harmony.

Straightforwardness: Clients ought to know when and how personalization is being applied. Straightforwardness in personalization endeavors assists work with trusting.

The Eventual fate of Personalization and Client Experiences

The fate of personalization and client experiences holds significantly more commitment. As innovation advances and information investigation turns out to be more modern, organizations will actually want to make progressively customized encounters. Here are a few patterns to look for:

Simulated intelligence and AI: Man-made consciousness and AI will play a steadily expanding job in personalization. These advancements can dissect tremendous measures of information continuously, offering dynamic and responsive personalization.

IoT Information: With the Web of Things (IoT), organizations will approach information from many associated gadgets. This information can give more far reaching client bits of knowledge and personalization amazing open doors.

Prescient Personalization: Expectant personalization will turn out to be more pervasive. Organizations will foresee client requirements and inclinations before clients even acknowledge them.

Hyper-Personalization: With the accessibility of fine-grained information, hyper-personalization will be the following boondocks. This implies fitting encounters at a singular level, not simply inside fragments.

Cross-Channel Personalization: Personalization will reach out across different client touchpoints, guaranteeing a predictable and fitted experience from sites to versatile applications to in-store visits.

4.3Risk Management and Fraud Prevention

In the present unique business scene, risk the board and misrepresentation avoidance have become crucial parts of an association's procedure. The coming of computerized innovation and the interconnected idea of worldwide business tasks have presented new dangers and weaknesses that require proactive measures to safeguard resources and notoriety. In this article, we will investigate the significance of hazard the board and misrepresentation anticipation, the developing idea of dangers, and the procedures utilized by organizations to alleviate these difficulties.

The Meaning of Hazard The executives

Risk the executives is the most common way of recognizing, surveying, and focusing on likely dangers or vulnerabilities that can influence an association's targets, resources, and notoriety. Successful gamble the executives permits organizations to expect and address possible difficulties, subsequently upgrading strength and independent direction.

Kinds of Dangers

Functional Dangers: These envelop gambles emerging from interior cycles, frameworks, and human mistake. Functional dangers can incorporate IT disappointments, inventory network disturbances, representative mistakes, and administrative consistence issues.

Monetary Dangers: Monetary dangers connect with the possible loss of capital or pay because of market variances, credit defaults, or liquidity requirements. Overseeing monetary dangers is pivotal for keeping up with monetary soundness.

Key Dangers: Vital dangers relate to vulnerabilities related with business methodologies and choices. These may incorporate market changes, rivalry, or the inability to adjust to new advancements and patterns.

Notoriety Dangers: Notoriety gambles include occasions or activities that could harm an association's picture and brand. This might incorporate item reviews, untrustworthy way of behaving, or information breaks.

The Advancing Idea of Dangers

The computerized age has acquainted new intricacies and difficulties with risk the executives. Specifically, organizations presently face the accompanying developing dangers:

Network protection Dangers: As associations depend more on advanced framework and information, they become powerless to digital dangers. Cyberattacks, information breaks, and ransomware assaults present huge dangers to business coherence and information security.

Administrative Dangers: With a rising number of guidelines and consistence necessities across businesses, associations should stay cautious in guaranteeing they comply to these norms. Rebelliousness can bring about lawful outcomes and monetary punishments.

Production network Dangers: Worldwide stock chains are unpredictable and interconnected, making organizations defenseless against interruptions brought about by international occasions, cataclysmic events, or monetary vacillations. The Coronavirus pandemic delineated the meaning of having tough store network procedures.

Misrepresentation Counteraction: The Requirement for Cautiousness

Misrepresentation is a conscious demonstration to bamboozle or control to accomplish unlawful or out of line monetary or individual increase. Misrepresentation can happen at different levels, including representative extortion, client misrepresentation, and outer misrepresentation, and it can significantly affect an association's monetary wellbeing and notoriety.

Normal Sorts of Extortion

Fiscal summary Extortion: This includes distorting an association's monetary wellbeing through misrepresented bookkeeping data or exchanges. It can prompt swelled benefits and offer costs, drawing in unwary financial backers.

Resource Misappropriation: This sort of extortion incorporates misappropriation, robbery, or abuse of organization resources or assets. Workers might control cost reports or misuse reserves.

Pay off and Debasement: Defilement inside an association can have huge legitimate and reputational outcomes. Pay-offs, payoffs, and untrustworthy strategic approaches can prompt lawful activity and harm an association's standing.

Digital Extortion: With the expansion of computerized exchanges and collaborations, digital misrepresentation has turned into a critical danger. This incorporates phishing plans, data fraud, and online tricks that target the two people and organizations.

Systems for Chance Administration and Misrepresentation Avoidance

Risk Appraisal: Distinguishing and evaluating chances is the most vital phase in risk the board. Organizations ought to direct standard gamble appraisals, taking into account inside and outside factors that could affect their tasks. This incorporates assessing the likelihood and expected effect of each gamble.

Consistence and Administration: To oversee administrative dangers, associations ought to lay out powerful consistence programs. This incorporates remaining refreshed on important regulations and guidelines, carrying out inside controls, and directing standard consistence reviews.

Network safety Measures: Execute powerful online protection measures to shield against digital dangers. This incorporates utilizing firewalls, encryption, interruption discovery frameworks, and representative preparation to forestall and answer cyber-attacks.

Production network Broadening: Diminish the gamble of store network disturbances by enhancing providers and keeping up with alternate courses of action. This includes recognizing basic parts or providers and creating elective obtaining techniques.

Worker Preparing: Instruct representatives about the dangers and outcomes of misrepresentation. This ought to remember preparing for distinguishing potential extortion markers, detailing components, and an accentuation on moral way of behaving.

Information Investigation and Observing: Utilize information examination apparatuses to persistently screen monetary exchanges and distinguish irregularities or expected misrepresentation. Information examination can distinguish dubious examples or strange exchanges progressively.

Informant Projects: Urge workers and partners to report doubts of misrepresentation or dishonest conduct through secret informant programs. These projects give a channel to revealing worries unafraid of reprisal.

The Job of Innovation in Extortion Avoidance

Innovation assumes a urgent part in current misrepresentation counteraction endeavors. Organizations influence progressed instruments and answers for recognize, forestall, and alleviate extortion chances. Here are a few vital mechanical developments around here:

AI and Man-made reasoning: These advances are utilized to dissect huge datasets and recognize designs related with deceitful way of behaving. AI models can consistently gain from information and work on their capacity to distinguish misrepresentation over the long run.

Blockchain Innovation: Blockchain gives a solid and straightforward record that can assist with forestalling extortion, particularly in monetary exchanges. It lessens the gamble of altering records and gives straightforwardness.

Biometric Confirmation: Biometric information, like unique mark or facial acknowledgment, is progressively utilized for secure admittance to frameworks, records, and gadgets. This adds an additional layer of safety to forestall unapproved access and data fraud.

Social Investigation: Conduct examination analyzes client conduct to recognize abnormalities. This is especially helpful in recognizing extortion in web-based exchanges. For instance, in the event that a client out of nowhere makes a bizarrely huge exchange, it might set off an extortion alert.

Continuous Observing: Constant checking of monetary exchanges, both in banking and online business, is critical to recognize and stop deceitful action as it happens. Frameworks can consequently signal and examine dubious exchanges.

Challenges in Misrepresentation Counteraction

While innovation has given significant devices to misrepresentation anticipation, it has likewise introduced new difficulties:

Refined Misrepresentation Methods: As hostile to extortion measures become further developed, fraudsters are continually advancing their strategies to sidestep security frameworks.

Security Concerns: Adjusting the requirement for strong misrepresentation avoidance with protection concerns is a continuous test. A few techniques, like broad information assortment and observation, may bring up moral issues.

Costs: Carrying out and keeping up with extortion avoidance innovation can be costly. Private companies might confront monetary requirements in taking on complex arrangements.

Client Experience: Offsetting security with a consistent client experience is a test. Excessively mind boggling safety efforts can baffle clients, possibly prompting lost business.

4.4Challenges and Opportunities

In both business and society, difficulties and potential open doors are entwined. Challenges test an association's versatility and development, while valuable open doors offer the potential for development and progress. As we explore the consistently advancing scene of the 21st hundred years, it's fundamental to comprehend the elements of difficulties and open doors and what they mean for different parts of our lives.

Challenges:

Monetary Vulnerability: Financial vulnerability, driven by factors like worldwide monetary movements, exchange debates, and the unconventionality of monetary business sectors, presents a huge test for organizations. It settles on long haul arranging and venture choices more troublesome.

Mechanical Disturbance: Quick innovative progressions can upset laid out enterprises and plans of action. Organizations should adjust or risk becoming old. This challenge is especially articulated in areas like retail, transportation, and money.

Environmental Change and Maintainability: Environmental change represents a significant test for legislatures, organizations, and society all in all. It requires proactive endeavors to alleviate its belongings, decrease fossil fuel byproducts, and change to manageable practices. Inability to address environmental change can prompt natural fiascoes and long haul financial precariousness.

Network safety Dangers: As organizations and people become more dependent on innovation, the danger of cyberattacks keeps on developing. Safeguarding touchy information and framework from digital dangers is a steady test. High-profile breaks can have serious results, including monetary misfortunes and reputational harm.

Social and Political Turmoil: Political and social unsteadiness, whether driven by imbalances, social strains, or international struggles, can disturb business tasks and broaderly affect society. Exploring these intricacies is an impressive test.

Amazing open doors:

Development and Innovation: Quick mechanical headways give various open doors to advancement. Organizations that embrace arising innovations like man-made brainpower, blockchain, and sustainable power can acquire an upper hand and drive development.

Worldwide Business sectors: With the development of worldwide business sectors, organizations have valuable chances to arrive at a more extensive client base. Internet business, for instance, permits organizations to take advantage of global business sectors, expanding their income potential.

Manageability and Green Works on: Embracing supportability can be a critical chance for organizations. Taking on harmless to the ecosystem practices could not just diminish an association's carbon impression at any point yet additionally draw in eco-cognizant buyers who support maintainable items and administrations.

Variety and Consideration: Embracing variety and incorporation in the work environment is a potential chance to take advantage of a more extensive ability pool, cultivate imagination, and take special care of different client socioeconomics. Comprehensive practices add to a more powerful and imaginative labor force.

Medical care and Biotechnology: Advances in medical services and biotechnology offer chances to work on human wellbeing and prosperity. Creating medicines and innovations to address wellbeing challenges, for example, accuracy medication and telehealth, can decidedly affect society.

The Interchange Among Difficulties and Open doors:

Advancement Because of Difficulties: Difficulties frequently drive development. At the point when organizations and society face major problems like environmental change and monetary vulnerability, they are incited to foster inventive arrangements. This advancement, thus, sets out new open doors for development.

Monetary and Cultural Flexibility: Confronting difficulties fabricates strength. Organizations that climate monetary slumps and different challenges are much of the time better prepared to immediately jump all over chances when they emerge. Flexibility permits organizations to adjust and flourish in evolving conditions.

Business Transformation: Fruitful organizations are those that perceive the two difficulties and valuable open doors. They adjust to difficulties, tracking down ways of relieving gambles and hold onto openings for development. An adaptable business procedure is fundamental for exploring the perplexing scene.

Cultural Advancement: Cultural advancement frequently happens because of difficulties. For instance, the social liberties development in the US and different regions of the planet arose as a reaction to fundamental difficulties connected with separation and disparity. These developments have made more comprehensive and just social orders.

Long haul Thinking: Adjusting difficulties and valuable open doors requires a drawn out point of view. Organizations and social orders that take on a ground breaking approach are bound to address difficulties successfully and influence open doors for enduring advancement.

Instances of Testing Amazing open doors:

Sustainable power: The test of environmental change has driven open doors in environmentally friendly power. As nations look to decrease fossil fuel byproducts, organizations in the environmentally friendly power area have developed dramatically. Sun oriented, wind, and hydroelectric power are becoming huge wellsprings of clean energy.

Telemedicine: The Coronavirus pandemic introduced the test of giving medical services while keeping up with social removing. This prompted the quick development of telemedicine, offering helpful and safe open doors for clinical interviews and care.

Remote Work: The test of the pandemic likewise sped up the remote work pattern. Organizations that embraced remote work valuable open doors guaranteed representative security as well as found the potential for cost investment funds and expanded efficiency.

Internet business and Advanced Change: The test of actual retail disturbances because of the ascent of internet business and changing shopper inclinations has set out open doors for organizations to put resources into computerized change. Organizations that adjust to online deals and advanced advertising can flourish in the computerized age.

Chapter 5

Artificial Intelligence And Machine Learning

Man-made reasoning (artificial intelligence) and AI (ML) are two of the most extraordinary innovations of the 21st 100 years. They have reshaped ventures, affected day to day existence, and are ready to reclassify what's in store. In this article, we'll investigate the ideas, applications, challenges, and the significant effect of simulated intelligence and ML.

Understanding Man-made brainpower and AI

Man-made consciousness alludes to the advancement of PC frameworks that can perform undertakings commonly requiring human insight. These undertakings incorporate critical thinking, regular language grasping, insight, and direction. Man-made intelligence can be additionally separated into two classes:

Limited simulated intelligence (or Powerless man-made intelligence): This type of computer based intelligence is intended for a particular errand or set of undertakings. Models incorporate remote helpers like Siri or Alexa, proposal frameworks like those on Netflix or Amazon, and chatbots for client care.

General man-made intelligence (or Solid simulated intelligence): This degree of artificial intelligence has the capacity to comprehend, learn, and play out any savvy task that a person would be able. Accomplishing this degree of computer based intelligence stays an objective of progressing innovative work.

AI, then again, is a subset of man-made intelligence that spotlights on the advancement of calculations and measurable models that empower PC frameworks to work on their exhibition on a particular errand through gaining from information. Rather than being expressly modified, ML models gain as a matter of fact and information. The educational experience can be ordered into three kinds:

Directed Learning: In this methodology, the model is prepared on marked information, implying that the calculation figures out how to anticipate or characterize information in view of models gave during preparing. It's generally expected utilized in errands like picture acknowledgment, language interpretation, and opinion examination.

Unaided Realizing: This type of learning manages unlabeled information. It's utilized to distinguish examples, bunches, or designs inside the information. Normal applications incorporate client division, peculiarity identification, and information pressure.

Support Learning: Support learning centers around navigation and control. Specialists advance by connecting with a climate, getting criticism as remunerations or disciplines for their activities. It is broadly utilized in advanced mechanics, game-playing computer based intelligence, and independent frameworks.

Utilizations of computer based intelligence and AI

Man-made intelligence and ML have had a tremendous effect across different businesses and spaces, generally changing the manner in which we live and work. Here are a portion of the remarkable applications:

Medical services: artificial intelligence and ML are changing medical services by supporting the finding of sicknesses, foreseeing patient results, and customizing therapy plans. Clinical imaging, drug disclosure, and telemedicine are regions encountering significant progressions.

Finance: In the monetary area, man-made intelligence and ML are utilized for misrepresentation location, algorithmic exchanging, risk appraisal, and client support chatbots. These advancements assist with further developing independent direction and decrease monetary dangers.

Retail: Online business organizations influence suggestion motors and client conduct investigation to give customized shopping encounters. Stock administration, estimating advancement, and request guaging have additionally profited from simulated intelligence and ML.

Fabricating: The utilization of computer based intelligence and ML has prompted upgraded prescient upkeep, process streamlining, and quality control in assembling. These innovations have made creation processes more proficient and financially savvy.

Independent Vehicles: simulated intelligence and ML are at the center of independent vehicles, empowering them to see their environmental elements, settle on continuous choices, and explore securely. This innovation can possibly upset transportation.

Normal Language Handling (NLP): NLP powers voice colleagues like Siri and Alexa, as well as chatbots and language interpretation administrations. It helps PCs comprehend and associate with human language.

Training: simulated intelligence is being utilized in schooling to make customized opportunities for growth, give computerized evaluating, and offer astute mentoring frameworks. This upgrades understudy commitment and scholastic results.

Security: man-made intelligence and ML assume a crucial part in online protection, assisting with identifying and answer dangers. They dissect examples of conduct to recognize dubious exercises and give constant insurance.

Farming: Accuracy agribusiness involves simulated intelligence and ML for soil examination, crop checking, and robotized collecting. This innovation augments crop yields and limits asset utilization.

The Effect of artificial intelligence and ML on Society

The reception of artificial intelligence and ML has prompted groundbreaking changes in the public eye:

Work Disturbance and Creation: man-made intelligence and ML have mechanized many errands, which can prompt labor force relocation in certain ventures. Be that as it may, they likewise set out new open doors in simulated intelligence advancement, information science, and the administration of computer based intelligence driven frameworks.

Further developed Medical care: The capacity of simulated intelligence to break down tremendous datasets and aid clinical conclusion can possibly save lives and further develop medical services results.

Personalization: man-made intelligence has empowered profoundly customized encounters in different spaces, from diversion and online business to medical services and schooling.

Proficiency and Efficiency: In the business world, artificial intelligence and ML have supported effectiveness and efficiency via mechanizing routine undertakings and offering experiences from enormous datasets.

Moral and Security Concerns: The utilization of man-made intelligence in direction can prompt predispositions and moral quandaries. As these advances are coordinated into different parts of life, it is crucial for address these worries.

Admittance to Data: man-made intelligence driven web search tools and suggestion frameworks give admittance to an abundance of data, upsetting how we access news, exploration, and diversion.

Ecological Effect: simulated intelligence and ML can be utilized to address natural difficulties, for example, environmental change and asset the executives, by upgrading energy use and lessening waste.

Difficulties and Contemplations

While the capability of computer based intelligence and ML is tremendous, there are additionally huge difficulties and contemplations:

Moral Worries: The utilization of computer based intelligence in navigation can prompt predispositions and moral quandaries. It's significant to guarantee that these frameworks are planned and checked to be fair and moral.

Information Protection: The huge measure of information expected to prepare man-made intelligence models raises worries about information security and security. Safeguarding individual and delicate data is a first concern.

Guideline and Oversight: As simulated intelligence and ML become more necessary to different businesses, administrative systems should be laid out to oversee their utilization and moderate possible dangers.

Straightforwardness and Logic: The "discovery" nature of some man-made intelligence models can go with it hard to comprehend their choice making processes. Guaranteeing straightforwardness and logic is a basic test.

Work Dislodging: Computerization and man-made intelligence driven frameworks can possibly upset work in specific areas. Setting up the labor force for these progressions is a squeezing challenge.

Constant Learning: simulated intelligence and ML models require progressing learning and transformation. Guaranteeing that these frameworks stay cutting-edge and exact is a test.

The Eventual fate of computer based intelligence and ML

The eventual fate of computer based intelligence and ML is inconceivably encouraging. As these innovations keep on propelling, we can hope to see:

More Personalization: simulated intelligence frameworks will keep on giving profoundly customized encounters in regions like amusement, schooling, and medical services.

Upgraded Choice Help: computer based intelligence will turn into a crucial device for chiefs, giving experiences and proposals across a large number of spaces.

Independent Frameworks: Independent vehicles, robots, and robots will turn out to be more predominant, changing ventures like transportation and strategies.

Simulated intelligence in Exploration: computer based intelligence will assume a critical part in logical examination, helping with information examination, recreations, and the disclosure of new experiences.

Medical services Progressions: simulated intelligence and ML will keep on further developing medical care results by improving diagnostics, therapy plans, and medication revelation.

Natural Arrangements: computer based intelligence will be utilized to address ecological difficulties, for example, environmental change and asset the executives, by upgrading energy use and lessening waste.

Moral and Fair man-made intelligence: Endeavors to make artificial intelligence more moral and straightforward will keep, guaranteeing that these innovations are utilized capably.

5.1AI in Customer Service

Computerized reasoning (simulated intelligence) has been making critical advances into different enterprises, and one of its most extraordinary applications is in the domain of client assistance.

Computer based intelligence fueled advancements are reshaping the way in which organizations communicate with their clients, offering creative arrangements that upgrade the client experience. In this article, we will investigate the job of man-made intelligence in client support, its applications, advantages, challenges, and the eventual fate of this unique field.

The Job of computer based intelligence in Client care

Simulated intelligence is generally altering the manner in which organizations approach client care. Generally, client care has been to a great extent dependent on human specialists to address requests, tackle issues, and offer help. Notwithstanding, simulated intelligence advancements, including Regular Language Handling (NLP), AI, chatbots, and menial helpers, are currently computerizing numerous parts of client support.

Chatbots and Menial helpers: Chatbots are computer based intelligence driven applications that can reenact discussions with clients. They give continuous reactions to much of the time got clarification on pressing issues, help with essential critical thinking, and direct clients to the fitting assets. Remote helpers, similar to Amazon's Alexa or Apple's Siri, are further developed computer based intelligence frameworks that can perform errands and answer questions past client care, like setting updates, playing music, or controlling savvy gadgets.

NLP and Language Getting it: NLP permits man-made intelligence frameworks to comprehend and decipher human language. This innovation empowers chatbots and remote helpers to participate in regular, human-like discussions with clients, making collaborations more effective and customized.

Prescient Examination: computer based intelligence driven prescient investigation can assist organizations with expecting client needs and inclinations. By breaking down verifiable information and client conduct, computer based intelligence can make item proposals, send designated advertising offers, and work on strategically pitching and upselling methodologies.

Robotization and Self-Administration: simulated intelligence mechanizes routine errands and cycles in client care, for example, secret key resets, request following, and record the executives. This decreases the responsibility on human specialists, empowering them to zero in on more mind boggling and high-esteem client collaborations.

Utilizations of simulated intelligence in Client support

Man-made intelligence has a large number of utilizations in client care, upgrading different parts of the client venture:

Virtual Specialists and Chatbots: artificial intelligence controlled virtual specialists can deal with client requests and give moment reactions. They are accessible all day, every day and can deal with a high volume of questions all the while, guaranteeing clients get convenient help. Whether it's responding to much of the time got clarification on some things, handling orders, or investigating issues, chatbots are an important resource in offering productive and steady help.

Customized Client Encounters: simulated intelligence investigates client information to make customized encounters. By figuring out a client's buy history, inclinations, and conduct, organizations can give custom-made item proposals, advancements, and content. This personalization upgrades consumer loyalty and drives deals.

Robotized Tagging and Directing: artificial intelligence can arrange and course client requests to the most proper human specialist or group. This guarantees that issues are tended to by the right subject matter experts, lessening reaction times and upgrading issue goal.

Opinion Examination: computer based intelligence can break down client criticism and feeling progressively. By checking online entertainment, client audits, and reviews, organizations can acquire experiences into client insights and address issues immediately. Opinion investigation permits organizations to recognize regions for development and pursue information driven choices.

Email and Text Computerization: artificial intelligence driven frameworks can robotize email reactions and text informing. They can answer normal inquiries, affirm orders, and give request following data without human intercession. This computerization smoothes out correspondence and further develops proficiency.

Voice Partners: simulated intelligence voice collaborators, similar to those in brilliant speakers and cell phones, give without hands client assistance. Clients can ask about items, administrations, and data, empowering organizations to expand their range and availability.

Advantages of artificial intelligence in Client assistance

The reception of artificial intelligence in client assistance offers a few key benefits:

all day, every day Accessibility: computer based intelligence driven chatbots and remote helpers are accessible nonstop, guaranteeing clients can get support whenever. This is especially gainful for worldwide organizations with clients in various time regions.

Proficiency and Speed: simulated intelligence can deal with client requests quickly and with consistency. There are no deferrals because of specialist accessibility, and routine undertakings are robotized, decreasing reaction times.

Versatility: simulated intelligence can deal with a high volume of requests all the while. As organizations develop, they can scale their client support tasks without essentially employing more human specialists.

Personalization: simulated intelligence investigates client information to give customized proposals and offers. This personalization further develops consumer loyalty and reliability.

Cost Decrease: Via robotizing routine errands and lessening the responsibility on human specialists, computer based intelligence can prompt expense reserve funds in client care tasks.

Further developed Information Bits of knowledge: man-made intelligence driven examination give significant experiences into client conduct, inclinations, and fulfillment levels. This information can illuminate advertising systems, item advancement, and by and large business choices.

Upgraded Issue Goal: computer based intelligence frameworks can help human specialists in critical thinking by giving important data and assets, assisting specialists with resolving complex issues all the more successfully.

Difficulties and Contemplations

While man-made intelligence in client care offers various advantages, it additionally accompanies its own arrangement of difficulties and contemplations:

Absence of Human Touch: A few clients might incline toward interfacing with human specialists, especially for complicated or intense subject matters. Finding some kind of harmony among robotization and human cooperation is critical.

Information Protection: Taking care of client information requires a hearty information insurance structure to guarantee protection and security. Organizations should conform to information protection guidelines and keep up with the trust of their clients.

Coordination with Existing Frameworks: Incorporating man-made intelligence frameworks with existing client assistance foundation can be mind boggling. Similarity issues and information relocation difficulties might emerge during execution.

Introductory Expenses: Creating and carrying out simulated intelligence frameworks can include forthright expenses. Be that as it may, the drawn out benefits frequently offset these underlying speculations.

Preparing and Observing: Preparing simulated intelligence models and checking their exhibition is a continuous interaction. Customary updates and changes are important to guarantee that the innovation stays powerful.

Moral Contemplations: Guaranteeing that computer based intelligence frameworks settle on moral and unprejudiced choices is a basic test. Predisposition in artificial intelligence frameworks can prompt separation and adversely influence client encounters.

Client Acknowledgment: A few clients might be careful about computer based intelligence in client assistance. Viable correspondence and training are important to fabricate trust and acknowledgment.

The Fate of simulated intelligence in Client support

The fate of simulated intelligence in client assistance is ready to be dynamic and extraordinary. Here are a few patterns and improvements to look for:

Half and half Models: The coordination of artificial intelligence and human specialists is probably going to turn out to be more refined. Organizations will foster cross breed client care models that join the proficiency of computer based intelligence with the sympathy and critical abilities to think of people.

High level NLP: Upgrades in NLP innovation will make artificial intelligence frameworks much more proficient at understanding and answering regular language.

Discussions with simulated intelligence will turn out to be progressively consistent and human-like.

Man-made intelligence Upgraded Examination: artificial intelligence driven examination will give further bits of knowledge into client conduct, empowering organizations to pursue more educated choices progressively.

Man-made intelligence Empowered Omnichannel Backing: man-made intelligence will empower steady and customized help across different client collaboration channels, like talk, email, telephone, and virtual entertainment.

Computer based intelligence Fueled Voice Collaborators: Voice-actuated menial helpers will keep on advancing, offering organizations more open doors for without hands client communications.

Artificial intelligence Supported Information Bases: simulated intelligence driven information bases will upgrade self-administration choices, giving clients speedy and exact answers for their requests.

Moral simulated intelligence Advancement: Organizations will focus on moral man-made intelligence improvement, zeroing in on reasonableness, straightforwardness, and decreasing predisposition in client support cooperations.

5.2Predictive Analytics

Prescient investigation is a progressive field that utilizes information, calculations, and measurable displaying to conjecture future occasions or patterns. It rises above conventional information examination by utilizing verifiable information to give important bits of knowledge about what lies ahead. This unique innovation has acquired massive unmistakable quality, affecting ventures in all cases, and changing the manner in which associations decide and anticipate what's in store.

Prescient investigation includes a few fundamental stages, starting with information assortment and preprocessing. This interaction involves assembling and cleaning information from different sources, guaranteeing it's reasonable for examination. Include choice is the following critical stage, as it includes distinguishing the most persuasive factors that will direct expectations.

When the information is prepared, it is basic to choose a fitting prescient model. This model can go from basic straight relapse to complex AI calculations, contingent upon the idea of the information and the expectation job needing to be done. The model is then prepared utilizing verifiable information to recognize examples and connections inside the information. Subsequent to preparing, the model's presentation is assessed to guarantee its exactness and dependability.

Prescient examination tracks down applications across a large number of enterprises, offering a flexible and priceless device for associations. In advertising and client relationship the board, it empowers organizations to grasp client conduct, foresee their inclinations, and improve promoting efforts. It assumes a critical part in monetary administrations by surveying credit risk, distinguishing extortion, and improving speculation procedures. In medical services, prescient examination helps with illness flare-up forecast, patient consideration, and early mediation, at last saving lives.

The retail business tackles prescient examination for request determining, stock administration, and client experiences. It upgrades fabricating cycles and inventory network the board, diminishing waste and further developing proficiency. Prescient examination additionally tracks down its place in energy and utilities, where it advances energy utilization and predicts hardware disappointments, adding to cost reserve funds and supportability.

HR offices utilize prescient investigation for ability securing, labor force arranging, and distinguishing representative weakening dangers, while telecom organizations influence it to upgrade network execution and lessen client stir. Indeed, even in the realm of sports, prescient examination has turned into an important resource, supporting execution investigation and injury expectation.

Prescient examination utilizes different philosophies and procedures, including relapse investigation, choice trees, AI calculations, time series investigation, bunching, and grouping. These strategies are picked in view of the idea of the information and the particular prescient undertaking. As information proceeds to develop and advance, the strategies utilized in prescient examination adjust to address the difficulties and intricacies of contemporary information sources.

In spite of the various benefits of prescient examination, it accompanies its own arrangement of difficulties. The nature of information assumes an essential part in the precision of expectations. Loud, fragmented, or one-sided information can prompt wrong outcomes, making information quality a foremost concern.

Overfitting, a typical test in prescient displaying, happens when a model is excessively perplexing and fits the preparation information impeccably however battles to sum up to new, concealed information. Model choice can be an overwhelming errand, as the exhibition of various models might change relying upon the dataset and the front and center concern. Information protection and security concerns should be tended to while dealing with delicate client information, and it is fundamental to keep up with trust.

Interpretable models are inclined toward in applications where straightforwardness is essential, as a few prescient models, particularly profound learning models, can be trying to decipher. Model support is a continuous prerequisite, as models require standard updates to stay precise and pertinent.

Moral contemplations are fundamental in prescient examination. Guaranteeing that models are liberated from inclination and moral worries is a basic test, as one-sided forecasts can prompt segregation and moral quandaries.

The effect of prescient examination is significant, impacting different parts of our advanced world. It improves direction by giving information driven bits of knowledge, mitigates takes a chance by distinguishing expected issues ahead of time, and upgrades asset designation, decreasing expenses and improving proficiency. Prescient investigation has likewise prompted better client encounters through customized suggestions and designated promoting. In medical care, it helps with early sickness recognition and medication improvement, offering the possibility to save lives.

Prescient investigation likewise adds to ecological manageability by anticipating catastrophic events and upgrading asset use. It improves security estimates in transportation and flight by anticipating mishaps and hardware disappointments.

The future of prescient examination is promising, with a few patterns and improvements not too far off. Reasonable man-made intelligence will be a point of convergence, giving straightforward and fathomable models that can make sense of their forecasts. Ongoing forecasts will turn out to be progressively crucial in a universe of moment information, especially in spaces like online protection, money, and web based business. Robotized AI (AutoML) instruments will work on the demonstrating system, making prescient investigation open to a more extensive crowd.

The joining of prescient investigation with the Web of Things (IoT) will take into consideration the continuous observing and prescient support of IoT gadgets, further improving tasks. Moral contemplations will keep on acquiring significance, with associations zeroing in on decency, straightforwardness, and predisposition decrease. Prescient examination will play a steadily expanding job in medical services, reforming patient consideration and medication improvement.

Cross-industry reception of prescient examination will keep on extending, as associations perceive driving development and gain an upper hand potential. In this period of information driven bits of knowledge, prescient examination is a groundbreaking power that prepares associations to pursue informed choices and get ready for the future with certainty. An innovation keeps on forming the cutting edge world and will without a doubt assume a critical part in the years to come.

5.3AI in Investment and Wealth Management

Man-made brainpower (simulated intelligence) is upsetting the universe of speculation and abundance the board, disturbing customary practices and offering additional opportunities for financial backers and monetary establishments. This innovation, portrayed by AI, information investigation, and prescient demonstrating, is rethinking the way that monetary experts go with speculation choices, oversee portfolios, and give customized counsel to clients. In this article, we will investigate the applications, advantages, challenges, and the fate of simulated intelligence in venture and abundance the board.

Artificial intelligence Applications in Venture and Abundance The executives

Algorithmic Exchanging: computer based intelligence driven algorithmic exchanging frameworks utilize authentic and ongoing information to execute trade orders. These calculations can rapidly deal with huge measures of data, distinguish market drifts, and execute exchanges at ideal times. Thusly, they look to outflank conventional human exchanging procedures.

Portfolio The board: computer based intelligence is utilized to make and oversee speculation portfolios. It examines verifiable information, market patterns, and the singular financial backer's objectives and chance resilience to construct a broadened portfolio customized to their necessities.

Robo-Counsels: Robo-guides are mechanized stages that utilization computer based intelligence to give monetary exhortation and oversee ventures for clients. They survey what is happening and hazard profile, then, at that point, suggest and deal with an arrangement of resources. Robo-consultants offer minimal expense arrangements, making abundance the board more open to a more extensive crowd.

Risk Appraisal: computer based intelligence frameworks survey speculation takes a chance by investigating market information and monetary pointers. They can distinguish possible dangers and give early admonitions, empowering financial backers to settle on informed choices.

Extortion Recognition: computer based intelligence is utilized to distinguish deceitful exercises inside monetary exchanges. By dissecting examples and abnormalities in exchange information, it can recognize likely occurrences of extortion and caution monetary establishments.

Client Bits of knowledge: simulated intelligence frameworks examine client information to acquire experiences into financial backer way of behaving, inclinations, and necessities. This data assists monetary foundations with offering more customized types of assistance and designer their contributions to individual clients.

Advantages of man-made intelligence in Venture and Abundance The executives

Effectiveness: computer based intelligence calculations can deal with huge measures of information and perform complex examinations like a flash, which is past the capacities of human financial backers. This effectiveness can prompt more educated venture choices.

Risk The board: computer based intelligence distinguishes possible dangers and market vacillations, empowering financial backers to go to proactive lengths to safeguard their portfolios. It offers further developed risk appraisal and alleviation.

Enhancement: computer based intelligence can make very much expanded speculation portfolios by considering a wide scope of resources and economic situations. Enhancement decreases gambles and further develop returns.

Lower Expenses: Robo-consultants and computerized exchanging frameworks frequently have lower charges contrasted with conventional human guides. This cost-viability makes abundance the board benefits more open to a more extensive scope of financial backers.

Personalization: artificial intelligence driven frameworks can offer exceptionally customized speculation exhortation and portfolio the executives in view of individual client needs, risk resilience, and monetary objectives.

Deadpan Navigation: man-made intelligence calculations are not affected by feelings or inclinations, which can influence human venture choices. They go with choices in light of information and examination as opposed to dread or avarice.

Difficulties and Contemplations

In spite of its many benefits, the reception of simulated intelligence in speculation and abundance the executives isn't without its difficulties:

Information Security and Security: Overseeing delicate monetary information requires vigorous safety efforts to safeguard against information breaks and digital dangers. Keeping up with client trust is central.

Administrative Consistence: Monetary foundations should explore a complex administrative scene while executing artificial intelligence in their tasks. Consistence with guidelines like GDPR, HIPAA, and monetary industry-explicit principles is vital.

Moral Worries: Guaranteeing that artificial intelligence frameworks settle on moral choices and stay away from predisposition in venture proposals is a huge test. Accidental predisposition in artificial intelligence models can prompt prejudicial results.

Human Oversight: While computer based intelligence can give important bits of knowledge and help, human oversight stays fundamental, especially for high-stakes speculation choices. Finding some kind of harmony between human ability and simulated intelligence support is basic.

Interpretability: Some artificial intelligence models, especially profound learning models, can be challenging to decipher. Monetary experts need to comprehend and believe the choices made by computer based intelligence frameworks.

The Eventual fate of simulated intelligence in Speculation and Abundance The executives

The fate of artificial intelligence in speculation and abundance the executives is brimming with potential outcomes and advancements. Here are a few patterns and improvements to look for:

High level AI: man-made intelligence calculations will turn out to be more complex, empowering better forecasts and more exact speculation systems. Profound learning and support learning will assume a more noticeable part in portfolio the board and chance evaluation.

Reasonable simulated intelligence: The requirement for straightforwardness and interpretability in artificial intelligence models will prompt the advancement of logical man-made intelligence. This permits monetary experts to comprehend and believe the choices made by computer based intelligence frameworks.

Crossover Models: The coordination of human skill with computer based intelligence help will turn out to be more predominant. Monetary experts will utilize artificial intelligence instruments to improve their dynamic cycles, joining the qualities of the two people and machines.

Expanded Guideline: As computer based intelligence assumes a more critical part in the monetary area, administrative bodies will probably acquaint new guidelines and rules with guarantee moral and fair simulated intelligence use.

Computer based intelligence Fueled Monetary Items: Monetary organizations might present simulated intelligence driven monetary items that adjust to economic situations continuously, furnishing clients with more unique and customized speculation choices.

Moral and Fair artificial intelligence: Guaranteeing moral simulated intelligence use and lessening predisposition in speculation suggestions will stay a need. Monetary establishments will put resources into dependable computer based intelligence improvement.

5.4Ethical Concerns

In the quickly advancing computerized age, moral worries have become progressively conspicuous. As innovation keeps on changing our reality, from man-made brainpower and biotechnology to information protection and natural issues, moral contemplations are vital. This article dives into the moral worries emerging from innovative progressions, featuring the requirement for moral structures, mindful turn of events, and cultural attention to explore the intricate moral scene of the 21st 100 years.

Information Protection and Security

One of the first moral worries in the advanced age spins around information protection and security. The inescapable assortment, investigation, and usage of individual information have brought up issues about individual independence and the potential for misuse. With web-based entertainment stages, internet business sites, and different applications gathering broad information on clients, the gamble of information breaks and unapproved access is a steady concern.

Guaranteeing that individual information is treated with extreme attention to detail and defending against cyberattacks and information robbery is a basic moral commitment. Controllers and associations should lay out severe information security measures, and people ought to be proactive in understanding how their information is utilized and upholding for their protection privileges.

Man-made reasoning and Inclination

Man-made reasoning (simulated intelligence) has progressed quickly, raising critical moral worries. One of the most major problems is the potential for predisposition in man-made intelligence frameworks. AI models prepared on one-sided or unrepresentative information can propagate or try and worsen cultural predispositions. For instance, one-sided artificial intelligence calculations in recruiting cycles can prompt victimization explicit segment gatherings.

Addressing these moral worries requires fastidious consideration regarding information quality, straightforwardness, and reasonableness in man-made intelligence improvement. Different and agent datasets, moral simulated intelligence plan, and constant observing are imperative to guarantee that computer based intelligence frameworks don't build up destructive predispositions.

Independent Frameworks and Moral Navigation

The advancement of independent frameworks, including self-driving vehicles and military robots, presents interesting moral quandaries. These frameworks should pursue split-subsequent options that can have life-and-demise results, bringing up issues about how they ought to focus on human wellbeing, moral standards, and the potential for accidental mischief.

The moral advancement of independent frameworks requests the foundation of clear rules and dynamic structures. Guaranteeing straightforwardness in how these frameworks work and making them responsible for their activities is crucial for gain cultural trust.

Biotechnology and Hereditary Designing

Biotechnology, especially hereditary designing, can possibly upset medical services and farming. Nonetheless, it likewise acquaints significant moral worries related with quality altering and its suggestions. For instance, CRISPR-Cas9 innovation empowers exact hereditary changes however could prompt unseen side-effects or moral situations, for example, fashioner children.

Adjusting the commitment of biotechnology with moral contemplations requires severe oversight, clear moral rules, and worldwide collaboration. Open discourse among researchers, policymakers, and general society is pivotal to deciding the limits of mindful hereditary designing.

Ecological and Environment Concerns

Innovative headways frequently accompany ecological and environment suggestions. The moral concern lies in the ecological effect of innovation, especially regarding fossil fuel byproducts, asset exhaustion, and electronic waste. The advanced age's dependence on energy-concentrated server farms, gadgets assembling, and quick oldness brings up issues about supportability.

Tending to these moral worries includes taking on maintainable works on, lessening e-squander, and changing to sustainable power sources. Stricter guidelines and corporate obligation in limiting ecological effect are likewise fundamental.

Work and Computerization

The computerization of occupations and the ascent of man-made brainpower in the work environment raise moral worries about business and laborers' freedoms. The uprooting of human laborers by machines, while possibly expanding proficiency, may prompt monetary disparity, joblessness, and a deficiency of occupation fulfillment.

Moral arrangements include setting up the labor force for the computerized age through retraining and reskilling programs. Moreover, general essential pay and creative work strategies might be important to guarantee that the advantages of computerization are impartially conveyed.

Moral Structures and Rules

To address these moral worries successfully, the improvement of moral structures and rules is urgent. Such structures can give an outline to moral dynamic in different fields. For example, clinical morals and bioethics give standards and rules to medical services experts and specialists to explore complex moral situations.

In the domain of innovation, associations and policymakers are progressively perceiving the significance of moral man-made intelligence standards. The improvement of simulated intelligence morals rules, like those by the European Association and the OECD, stresses the upsides of straightforwardness, responsibility, decency, and human-driven artificial intelligence advancement. These standards mean to guarantee that computer based intelligence innovations line up with cultural qualities and don't disregard common freedoms or support destructive inclinations.

Dependable Turn of events and Advancement

Mindful turn of events and development require a proactive obligation to moral contemplations. Innovation organizations, research establishments, and government offices ought to integrate morals into their innovative work processes. They ought to focus on moral surveys, variety in research groups, and consistent evaluation of innovation's effect on society.

Besides, the reception of moral plan rehearses, like security by-plan and decency by-plan, can assist with alleviating expected moral worries from the start of innovation improvement.

Cultural Mindfulness and Training

Upgrading cultural mindfulness and schooling about moral worries is crucial. Public talk and commitment can shape moral conversations and impact innovative turn of events. An educated society is better prepared to consider associations and policymakers responsible for moral failures.

Instructive organizations play a vital part in setting up the up and coming age of innovation experts and residents. Courses and educational plans zeroed in on morals in innovation can impart major areas of strength for an establishment in later trendsetters and pioneers.

Worldwide Coordinated effort and Guideline

In an interconnected world, moral worries frequently rise above public boundaries. In this manner, worldwide cooperation and guideline are important to address worldwide moral difficulties. Arrangements, principles, and shows can assist with blending moral methodologies and guarantee that innovation regards major common liberties and values.

Endeavors to make peaceful accords, similar to the Paris Arrangement for environmental change, are characteristic of the worldwide local area's obligation to tending to shared moral worries.

Chapter 6

The Role Of Cybersecurity

In the present interconnected world, where computerized innovation has turned into a fundamental piece of our lives, the job of online protection is more basic than any time in recent memory. As organizations, states, and people depend on computerized stages and organizations for correspondence, business, and data sharing, the need to safeguard delicate information and framework from digital dangers is principal. This article investigates the advancing job of online protection in shielding the computerized scene, tending to the difficulties, systems, and its developing importance in the cutting edge age.

The Advanced Change and Its Difficulties

The quick development of innovation has introduced the time of computerized change. With the multiplication of the web, distributed computing, and the Web of Things (IoT), we have seen exceptional network and information trade. While this has brought tremendous advantages, it has likewise uncovered weaknesses that vindictive entertainers try to take advantage of.

Cyberattacks, information breaks, and online dangers have turned into a consistent concern. These assaults come in different structures, including malware, phishing, ransomware, and Dispersed Disavowal of Administration (DDoS) assaults. They target people, associations, and, surprisingly, basic foundation, prompting monetary misfortunes, information robbery, and possible disturbances.

The Job of Network safety in Safeguarding Information

Network safety assumes a critical part in safeguarding information, quite possibly of the most important resource in the computerized age. It envelops different measures and practices intended to protect information honesty, secrecy, and accessibility. These include:

Information Encryption: Encryption changes information into a protected configuration that must be perused with the legitimate unscrambling key. It is an essential part of getting information during transmission and capacity.

Access Control: Access control components guarantee that main approved people or frameworks can get to delicate information. This forestalls unapproved access or information spillage.

Confirmation and Approval: Network safety frameworks utilize verification to check the character of clients and approval to allow or confine their entrance in view of jobs and consents.

Information Reinforcements: Customary information reinforcements and calamity recuperation plans are fundamental to moderate information misfortune in case of a break or framework disappointment.

Interruption Discovery and Counteraction Frameworks (IDS/IPS): These frameworks screen networks for dubious action and can consequently answer dangers, for example, obstructing an IP address engaged with a cyberattack.

Firewalls: Firewalls go about as a boundary between a confided in network and untrusted outside organizations, separating approaching and active organization traffic in view of predefined security rules.

Weakness Evaluation and Fix The board: Customary weakness appraisals and convenient programming refreshes help recognize and fix shortcomings that could be taken advantage of by cybercriminals.

Safeguarding Basic Framework

Basic foundation, including power matrices, water treatment plants, and transportation frameworks, depends intensely on computerized advancements. The job of network safety in safeguarding these essential frameworks couldn't possibly be more significant. A fruitful cyberattack on basic foundation can have deplorable outcomes.

To safeguard basic framework, hearty online protection measures are required. These may incorporate air-gapped networks, which are actually separated from the web, severe access controls, and persistent observing for any surprising movement.

Online protection in the Business World

Organizations, both huge and little, rely upon computerized frameworks for tasks, information capacity, and client associations.

Network safety is vital in safeguarding business resources, keeping up with client trust, and guaranteeing consistence with information security guidelines. The job of online protection in the business world envelops a few key perspectives:

Risk The executives: Organizations should recognize expected dangers and weaknesses in their advanced foundation and focus on network safety gauges in like manner.

Episode Reaction: in case of a network safety occurrence, associations need a distinct occurrence reaction intend to limit harm, recuperate information, and reestablish typical tasks.

Worker Preparing: Network protection preparing and mindfulness programs are fundamental to instruct representatives about accepted procedures, social designing dangers, and how to perceive phishing endeavors.

Consistence and Guidelines: Organizations should consent to information security and network safety guidelines, which change by area and industry. Resistance can bring about extreme monetary punishments.

Outsider Gamble: Organizations frequently team up with outsider merchants and specialist co-ops. The job of network protection reaches out to evaluating and dealing with the network protection practices of these accomplices to forestall production network weaknesses.

The Job of Legislatures and Public Network safety

States play a huge part in network safety, especially with regards to protecting public safety and basic framework. They are answerable for laying out and implementing network protection guidelines, answering digital dangers, and cultivating worldwide participation.

Key government online protection capabilities include:

Public Network protection Techniques: States foster procedures to address the advancing danger scene, framing arrangements, guidelines, and assets committed to network protection.

Policing: implementation organizations examine cybercrimes and seek after cybercriminals. This incorporates worldwide participation to capture cybercriminals working across borders.

Basic Framework Insurance: States work to get and safeguard basic foundation, guaranteeing that fundamental administrations are not undermined by cyberattacks.

Data Sharing: States work with data dividing among public and confidential areas to assist associations with remaining informed about arising dangers and weaknesses.

Network protection Schooling and Labor force Improvement: Legislatures frequently put resources into drives to prepare and foster an online protection labor force to satisfy the developing need for gifted experts.

Worldwide Joint effort

Digital dangers are not restricted by public lines. Worldwide coordinated effort assumes a critical part in tending to the worldwide idea of cyberattacks. Associations like INTERPOL, Europol, and the Unified Countries assist with working with global participation in battling cybercrime and advancing network safety best practices.

The Fate of Network protection

The job of online protection is ceaselessly developing to stay up with the quickly changing computerized scene. A few patterns and improvements will shape the fate of network protection:

Man-made reasoning and AI: simulated intelligence and AI are being utilized in online protection to recognize and answer dangers continuously. They can examine immense measures of information to recognize examples and inconsistencies, further developing danger identification.

Zero Trust Security: The conventional border based security model is giving method for focusing trust, which expects to be that nobody, whether inside or outside the organization, can be relied upon. Zero trust centers around severe character check and persistent observing.

Quantum Registering Dangers: The approach of quantum processing presents new difficulties to encryption techniques right now being used. Post-quantum cryptography will be critical to defend information in the quantum period.

IoT Security: With the multiplication of IoT gadgets, getting the extending assault surface is fundamental. IoT security principles and practices will keep on creating.

Network safety Regulation: As digital dangers become more modern, legislatures will sanction extra network safety regulation and guidelines to safeguard basic foundation and information.

Moral Hacking and Bug Abundance Projects: Associations will progressively draw in moral programmers and send off bug abundance projects to proactively distinguish and address weaknesses.

6.1Cyber Threats in Banking

The financial business has gone through critical change as of late, with the reception of computerized innovations and online administrations turning into the standard. While these headways have smoothed out tasks and further developed client comfort, they have likewise presented monetary establishments to a developing exhibit of digital dangers. From information breaks and ransomware assaults to phishing tricks and insider dangers, banks are continually in danger. In this article, we will investigate the different digital dangers looked by the financial area, their suggestions, and the procedures utilized to safeguard monetary foundations and their clients.

The Developing Scene of Digital Dangers

As the monetary business embraces digitalization, it has opened new roads for cybercriminals to take advantage of weaknesses. These dangers include many strategies, methods, and inspirations. Here are probably the most common digital dangers in banking:

1. **Phishing Assaults**
   Phishing is a misleading procedure where cybercriminals imitate genuine elements to fool people into uncovering delicate data, for example, login qualifications, Visa subtleties, and individual ID. Phishing assaults can happen through email, instant messages, virtual entertainment, or even calls. These assaults frequently target bank clients, endeavoring to acquire unapproved admittance to their records.
2. **Ransomware**
   Ransomware is a kind of malware that scrambles the casualty's information, delivering it difficult to reach until a payment is paid to the aggressor. Banking foundations are appealing focuses for ransomware assaults because of the potential for monetary benefit and the basic idea of their information. Effective

assaults can prompt critical monetary misfortunes and harm to the bank's standing.

3. **Insider Dangers**
   Insider dangers can emerge out of current or previous representatives, project workers, or colleagues with admittance to a bank's frameworks and information. These people may purposefully or accidentally compromise security. Insiders can take advantage of their admittance to commit misrepresentation, take information, or disturb tasks.
4. **Dispersed Disavowal of Administration (DDoS) Assaults**
   DDoS assaults flood a bank's site or organization with a gigantic volume of traffic, delivering administrations inaccessible to genuine clients. While DDoS assaults may not straightforwardly take information, they disturb tasks, possibly causing monetary misfortunes and harming client trust.
5. **Malware**
   Noxious programming, or malware, can taint a bank's frameworks, empowering cybercriminals to take delicate information, access records, and oversee network assets. Malware can be presented through email connections, downloads, or compromised sites.
6. **Data fraud**
   Data fraud includes taking individual and monetary data to commit deceitful exercises in a casualty's name. Monetary organizations are regularly focused on for fraud because of the abundance of individual information they have.
7. **Social Designing Assaults**

Social designing assaults maneuver people toward uncovering delicate data or making explicit moves. Cybercriminals frequently utilize mental control, trickery, or pantomime to take advantage of human way of behaving. These assaults can target bank workers or clients.

Ramifications of Digital Dangers in Banking

The ramifications of digital dangers in banking are expansive and can have serious ramifications for monetary organizations, their clients, and the more extensive economy:

Monetary Misfortunes: Effective cyberattacks can prompt significant monetary misfortunes for banks. These misfortunes can result from extortion, information breaks, the expense of researching and remediating the break, and likely fines and legitimate liabilities.

Notoriety Harm: Cyberattacks can seriously harm a bank's standing. Clients might lose trust in the foundation in the event that their own or monetary data is compromised. This deficiency of trust can prompt client wearing down and a decrease in new client acquisitions.

Functional Disturbance: DDoS assaults and ransomware occurrences can upset a bank's tasks, prompting administration blackouts, postponed exchanges, and burden for clients. Functional disturbances can bring about monetary misfortunes and administrative examination.

Administrative Consistence: Monetary establishments are dependent upon severe guidelines and consistence prerequisites. An information break or network safety occurrence can prompt administrative examinations, fines, and punishments for resistance.

Legitimate Outcomes: Banks might confront lawful activity from impacted clients or outsiders following a cyberattack. Legal claims, administrative activities, and authoritative debates can bring about huge lawful and monetary repercussions.

Client Effect: Cyberattacks can straightforwardly affect clients by undermining their monetary information or prompting data fraud. These episodes can cause profound trouble and monetary difficulty for people.

Safeguarding Against Digital Dangers in Banking

Relieving digital dangers in banking requires a multi-pronged methodology, joining innovation, cycles, and schooling. Here are systems monetary foundations utilize to safeguard against digital dangers:

Solid Validation: Carrying out strong multifaceted confirmation for clients and representatives can upgrade security. This expects clients to give various types of check prior to obtaining entrance.

Information Encryption: Encoding delicate information on the way and very still shields it from unapproved access even in case of a break.

Normal Programming Updates: Staying up with the latest is vital for fix known weaknesses. Cybercriminals frequently target obsolete or unpatched frameworks.

Worker Preparing: Exhaustive network safety preparing for representatives can help them perceive and answer phishing endeavors, social designing assaults, and different dangers. Instructed representatives are an imperative line of protection.

Access Controls: Executing severe access controls and guideline of least honor (giving clients just the base access required) can restrict the gamble of insider dangers.

Network Division: Sectioned networks separate delicate information from different frameworks, decreasing the gamble of sidelong development by aggressors inside the organization.

Episode Reaction Plans: Having a clear cut occurrence reaction plan set up assists monetary establishments with answering quickly to a cyberattack, limit harm, and reestablish typical tasks.

Joint effort: Sharing danger knowledge and teaming up with industry peers, government offices, and network protection specialists can assist manages an account with remaining informed about arising dangers.

Outsider Gamble The board: Surveying and checking the online protection practices of outsider sellers and specialist co-ops is fundamental to forestall production network weaknesses.

Administrative Consistence: Monetary foundations should comply to network safety guidelines and information insurance principles. Consistence isn't just a lawful prerequisite yet additionally an online protection best practice.

High level Danger Recognition: Utilizing progressed danger location arrangements, including interruption discovery and anticipation frameworks and security data and occasion the executives (SIEM) frameworks, can help recognize and answer digital dangers continuously.

The Advancing Idea of Digital Dangers

Digital dangers are consistently advancing as cybercriminals foster new strategies and strategies to break safety efforts. Along these lines, monetary foundations should stay watchful, adjust to arising dangers, and constantly further develop their network protection techniques.

Arising patterns in digital dangers in banking include:

Artificial intelligence and AI: Cybercriminals are utilizing simulated intelligence and AI to foster more complex and designated assaults. Banks should likewise use these innovations to upgrade their aggressive statement discovery abilities.

Store network Assaults: Aggressors are progressively focusing on outsider merchants and providers to get sufficiently close to their clients' frameworks. Banks should survey and moderate these store network weaknesses.

Zero-Day Weaknesses: Zero-day weaknesses are already obscure programming imperfections that assailants exploit before a fix is accessible. Banks need to remain watchful and utilize powerful weakness the board rehearses.

Digital money Related Dangers: The development of digital currencies has brought about dangers, for example, cryptojacking, ransomware assaults requesting cryptographic money installments, and fake introductory coin contributions (ICOs).

6.2Cybersecurity Technologies

In our interconnected world, online protection advances are the safeguards of the computerized domain. As innovation propels and pervades each part of our lives, the significance of safeguarding our information, frameworks, and organizations from digital dangers couldn't possibly be more significant. This article investigates the scene of online protection advancements, their developing job, and their importance in shielding our computerized resources.

1. **Antivirus and Against Malware Programming**

   Antivirus and hostile to malware programming are basic apparatuses in the online protection weapons store. They safeguard against realized dangers by checking documents and programming for malevolent code and examples. These advancements depend on broad information bases of known malware marks to distinguish and kill dangers. While compelling against deeply grounded dangers, they might battle with arising and refined malware.

2. **Firewalls**
   Firewalls are an essential part of organization security. They go about as an obstruction between a confided in network and untrusted outer organizations, separating approaching and active organization traffic in light of predefined security rules. Firewalls are fundamental for obstructing unapproved access and safeguarding network framework from dangers.
3. **Interruption Identification and Anticipation Frameworks (IDS/IPS)**
   Interruption identification and anticipation frameworks are intended to screen organization or framework exercises for vindictive or dubious way of behaving. IDSs recognize expected dangers, while IPSs make a move to hinder or relieve these dangers. They are basic for distinguishing and answering unapproved access, malware, and other security episodes.
4. **Encryption Advances**
   Encryption is the method involved with switching information into a solid organization over completely to forestall unapproved access. It is a foundation of information security, safeguarding delicate data during transmission and capacity. High level encryption advancements, like start to finish encryption, guarantee that main approved gatherings can translate the information.
5. **Multifaceted Confirmation (MFA)**
   Multifaceted confirmation adds an additional layer of safety by expecting clients to give at least two types of check prior to conceding access. This might incorporate something they know (e.g., a secret phrase), something they have (e.g., a cell phone), or something they are (e.g., biometric information). MFA mitigates the gamble of unapproved access regardless of whether one validation factor is compromised.
6. **Virtual Confidential Organizations (VPNs)**
   VPNs give a protected, encoded association for information transmission over untrusted networks, like the web. They guarantee information protection and privacy, making them important devices for telecommuters and secure correspondence.
7. **Security Data and Occasion The executives (SIEM) Frameworks**
   SIEM frameworks gather and investigate information from different sources, including network gadgets, servers, and security logs. They give ongoing observing and examination of safety occasions, permitting associations to immediately distinguish and answer dangers and irregularities.
8. **Fix The executives Apparatuses**
   Customary programming updates and fixes are fundamental for tending to known weaknesses in applications and working frameworks. Fix the board

apparatuses computerize the method involved with distinguishing and applying refreshes, lessening the window of openness to possible dangers.

9. **Secure Email Doors**
   Email is a typical vector for digital dangers, including phishing and malware dispersion. Secure email doors channel approaching and active email traffic, distinguishing and obstructing noxious substance, connections, and connections.
10. **Web Application Firewalls (WAFs)**
    Web application firewalls shield web applications from different dangers, including SQL infusion, cross-webpage prearranging (XSS), and different assaults. They assess and channel web traffic, impeding pernicious demands and traffic.
11. **Man-made brainpower (artificial intelligence) and AI (ML)**
    Man-made intelligence and ML advances assume a filling part in online protection. They examine immense datasets and examples to recognize dangers and inconsistencies, even those that are excessively perplexing for conventional mark based strategies. Computer based intelligence and ML can further develop danger location and reaction times.
12. **Conduct Examination**
    Conduct examination survey clients' or alternately substances' ways of behaving to distinguish deviations from typical action. This innovation can recognize insider dangers, uncommon record conduct, and other security occurrences.
13. **Endpoint Identification and Reaction (EDR) Arrangements**
    EDR arrangements center around safeguarding individual endpoints, like PCs, cell phones, and IoT gadgets. They screen these endpoints for dubious exercises, work with danger discovery, and answer episodes.
14. **Cloud Security Advancements**
    Cloud security advancements are intended to safeguard information and applications facilitated in cloud conditions. They incorporate personality and access the executives (IAM), encryption, and cloud security pose the board (CSPM) devices to get cloud resources.
15. **Web of Things (IoT) Security**
    With the expansion of IoT gadgets, it is fundamental to guarantee their security. IoT security advancements address the exceptional difficulties of getting associated gadgets, including verification, encryption, and gadget the executives.
16. **Danger Insight and Data Sharing**
    Danger insight administrations give convenient and important data about arising dangers and weaknesses. Associations can utilize this data to upgrade their security stance and danger reaction.
17. **Zero Trust Security Models**
    The zero trust model expects to be that nobody, whether inside or outside the organization, can be relied upon. It stresses severe character confirmation and

nonstop checking to guarantee that security stays strong in any event, when gadgets and clients are associated.

18. **Blockchain Innovation**

Blockchain is known for its application in digital currencies, however it likewise has security suggestions. Its decentralized and unchanging nature can improve information honesty and validation in different applications, including store network security and computerized personality.

Challenges and Developing Dangers

While network protection innovations have made considerable progress, the scene is continually advancing, introducing new difficulties and dangers:

High level Constant Dangers (APTs): APTs are refined and long haul cyber-attacks that explicitly target associations. They frequently include subtle, multi-stage goes after that are challenging to distinguish.

Social Designing: Cybercriminals keep on depending on human control to take advantage of people into uncovering delicate data or making explicit moves.

Computer based intelligence Upgraded Dangers: As man-made intelligence and ML innovations advance, so do digital dangers. Man-made intelligence driven assaults can be more versatile and successful in sidestepping conventional safety efforts.

Store network Assaults: Focusing on outsider sellers and providers has turned into an inexorably pervasive danger vector. Aggressors exploit weaknesses in the production network to think twice about target's security.

Digital Actual Assaults: As more basic framework becomes associated, the gamble of digital actual assaults, which control or disturb actual frameworks like power matrices or modern hardware, has developed.

6.3Regulatory Frameworks and Compliance

In an undeniably interconnected and information driven world, administrative structures and consistence assume a basic part in forming ventures, safeguarding purchasers, and keeping up with trust in different areas. These systems comprise of rules, norms, and rules laid out by states and administrative bodies to guarantee that organizations and associations work in a legitimate, moral, and responsible way. This article investigates the meaning of administrative structures and consistence, their effect on businesses, and the difficulties they present.

The Significance of Administrative Structures

Administrative structures serve a few critical capabilities in the cutting edge business scene:

Purchaser Security: Guidelines are intended to safeguard customers from unjustifiable practices, extortion, and inadequate items or administrations. These actions are especially fundamental in businesses where customers might miss the mark on data or assets to go with informed choices.

Market Dependability: Guidelines assist with keeping up with the soundness and trustworthiness of monetary business sectors. They lay out rules for exchanging, announcing, and exposure, forestalling market control and defending against foundational chances.

Ecological and General Wellbeing: Guidelines are fundamental in saving the climate and general wellbeing. They set guidelines for outflows, garbage removal, item security, and more to guarantee that organizations work dependably.

Information Protection and Security: During a time where information is a significant resource, guidelines connected with information protection and security have become progressively significant. They expect associations to shield delicate data, safeguard individual protection, and advise people if there should be an occurrence of information breaks.

Moral and Moral Principles: A few guidelines address moral and moral norms, especially in areas like medical services and examination, where choices can have critical moral ramifications.

Effect of Administrative Consistence

Consistence with administrative structures can significantly affect associations and enterprises:

Legitimate Outcomes: Inability to conform to guidelines can bring about lawful results, including fines, punishments, and expected legitimate activities from impacted parties.

Notoriety and Trust: Consistence improves an association's standing and encourages trust among clients, financial backers, and partners. Resistance can prompt reputational harm that is frequently difficult to recuperate from.

Functional Expenses: Following guidelines can increment functional expenses. Associations might have to put resources into consistence foundation, preparing, and reviews to guarantee adherence.

Advancement and Transformation: Administrative systems can energize or thwart development. While certain guidelines might smother innovativeness and contest, others can drive advancement by setting norms and offering impetuses for consistent practices.

Upper hand: Associations that show obligation to administrative consistence might acquire an upper hand. Consistence can be a selling point for organizations, particularly when customers esteem moral and dependable practices.

Challenges in Administrative Consistence

Exploring administrative systems and guaranteeing consistence isn't without its difficulties:

Intricacy: Administrative structures are frequently complicated and can fluctuate essentially by industry, ward, and topic. Grasping and complying with complex guidelines can be overpowering for associations.

Consistent Change: Guidelines are not static; they advance to address arising difficulties. Associations should remain informed about changes in guidelines and adjust their practices as needs be.

Globalization: Numerous associations work across borders, and that implies they should stick to a large number of administrative prerequisites. Globalization adds intricacy to consistence endeavors, as guidelines in various nations might struggle or cover.

Asset Requirements: More modest associations might miss the mark on assets expected to carry out far reaching consistence programs. Consistence frequently requests critical monetary and HR.

Interoperability: As innovation and information driven rehearses keep on extending, interoperability and information sharing guidelines become more significant. Guaranteeing consistence in information taking care of while as yet working with important data trade can be a difficult exercise.

Instances of Administrative Systems

A scope of administrative systems exists, each intended to address explicit worries and businesses. The following are a couple of prominent models:

Health care coverage Movability and Responsibility Act (HIPAA): HIPAA is a U.S. guideline that administers medical care information protection and security. It requires the insurance of patient data and sets rules for electronic wellbeing records.

General Information Insurance Guideline (GDPR): GDPR is an EU guideline that administers information security and assurance. It gives people more prominent command over their own information and forces severe prerequisites on organizations taking care of such information.

Sarbanes-Oxley Act (SOX): SOX is a U.S. government regulation that commands rigid monetary announcing and corporate administration practices to safeguard financial backers and guarantee the precision of budget summaries.

Basel III: Basel III is a worldwide administrative structure created by the Basel Board of trustees on Financial Management. It lays out principles for capital sufficiency, risk the executives, and liquidity chance to upgrade the soundness of the financial area.

Ecological Guidelines: Natural guidelines shift broadly and can resolve issues like discharges, squander the board, and asset preservation. The Ecological Security Office (EPA) in the US implements various natural guidelines.

The Job of Administrative Bodies

Administrative bodies are government offices or associations liable for making, carrying out, and upholding administrative systems. They assume an imperative part in guaranteeing that associations comply with the laid out rules and guidelines. Administrative bodies have a few key capabilities:

Strategy Advancement: Administrative bodies create and refresh guidelines to address current difficulties and worries in their separate areas.

Authorization: These bodies are answerable for checking consistence and implementing guidelines. They might direct reviews, examinations, and assessments to guarantee associations comply to the standards.

Schooling and Direction: Administrative bodies give direction and instruction to help associations comprehend and conform to guidelines. They frequently distribute consistence manuals and deal assets to help associations in their endeavors.

Information Assortment: Administrative bodies might gather information to survey the effect of guidelines and arrive at informed conclusions about future turns of events.

Question Goal: Administrative bodies frequently act as go betweens in debates connected with administrative consistence. They assist associations and people with settling issues through exchange or lawful cycles.

6.4The Ongoing Battle

Mankind has confronted a large number of worldwide difficulties over the entire course of time, going from pandemics and natural emergencies to social and political struggles. These continuous fights test our versatility, flexibility, and ability to team up even with difficulty. In this article, we will investigate probably the most squeezing worldwide provokes we proceed to defy and the endeavors made to address them.

1. **Worldwide Wellbeing Emergencies**
   Pandemics and worldwide wellbeing emergencies have forever been quite difficult for humankind. The Coronavirus pandemic, which started in late 2019, epitomizes the huge effect of a worldwide wellbeing emergency. This continuous fight against the infection has required worldwide participation, antibody dispersion, and general wellbeing endeavors to moderate its ramifications. The pandemic has uncovered the significance of readiness, the job of science, and the requirement for evenhanded admittance to medical services around the world.
2. **Environmental Change**
   Environmental change is an epic worldwide test that compromises the climate, economies, and the prosperity of people in the future. Climbing worldwide temperatures, outrageous climate occasions, and biodiversity misfortune are marks of this continuous fight. Peaceful accords like the Paris Understanding try to address environmental change by decreasing ozone harming substance emanations, progressing to feasible energy sources, and advancing dependable natural practices.
3. **Social Imbalance**
   Social imbalance, frequently determined by variations in pay, schooling, and admittance to assets, stays a diligent worldwide test. It is intently attached to issues of destitution, separation, and civil rights. Tending to social imbalance requires strategy changes, social mindfulness, and endeavors to connect the abundance hole through instruction, monetary changes, and inclusivity.

4. **Worldwide Relocation**
   The continuous development of individuals across borders and inside locales is a complex worldwide test. Factors like clash, financial open doors, and natural changes drive relocation. To address this test, nations need to foster extensive migration arrangements that offset security worries with compassionate necessities. It additionally requires worldwide participation to deal with the progression of dislodged populaces.
5. **Political Unsteadiness and Clashes**
   Political shakiness and clashes in different regions of the planet keep on disturbing lives and undermine worldwide harmony. Nationwide conflicts, provincial questions, and international pressures are mind boggling issues that request discretionary arrangements, peacekeeping endeavors, and the advancement of common liberties. The fight for soundness and harmony stays a first concern for worldwide associations, legislatures, and common society.
6. **Food Security**
   Guaranteeing food security for the developing worldwide populace is a consistent test. As the total populace increments, so does the requirement for dependable and maintainable food sources. The fight for food security requires developments in farming, dispersion, and impartial admittance to nourishment.
7. **Mechanical Progressions and Security**
   The fast speed of mechanical progressions has led to continuous fights concerning protection, information security, and moral utilization of innovation. Network protection dangers, information breaks, and worries about observation highlight the requirement for approaches and guidelines that offset development with individual freedoms.
8. **Admittance to Training**
   Admittance to quality training stays a continuous worldwide test. A huge number of youngsters and grown-ups need admittance to formal training because of financial variations, struggle, and deficient foundation. Guaranteeing instruction for everything is pivotal for individual turn of events, monetary development, and the strengthening of networks.
9. **Compassionate Emergencies and Exile Developments**
   Helpful emergencies, whether because of catastrophic events or clashes, bring about the dislodging of populaces and continuous outcast developments. The fight to give help, asylum, and backing to those impacted by these emergencies requires worldwide associations, NGOs, and legislatures to arrange their endeavors.
10. **Ecological Preservation**

The fight to moderate and safeguard the climate go on as human exercises put expanding tension on biological systems and regular assets. This continuous test calls for maintainable practices, preservation endeavors, and the mindful utilization of assets to protect the planet for people in the future.

Endeavors to Address Progressing Worldwide Difficulties

Tending to continuous worldwide difficulties requires aggregate endeavors from legislatures, global associations, common society, and people. Here are a portion of the techniques and drives pointed toward defying these difficulties:

Worldwide Participation: Numerous worldwide difficulties are transnational in nature and require global joint effort. Associations like the Unified Countries assume a focal part in cultivating collaboration and working with exchange among countries.

Examination and Development: Science and innovation assume an essential part in tending to worldwide difficulties. Exploration and advancement are fundamental in finding answers for issues like environmental change, pandemics, and food security.

Strategy and Regulation: States should establish approaches and regulation that address worldwide difficulties. Models incorporate natural guidelines, medical care approaches, and regulations pointed toward decreasing disparity.

Compassionate Guide and Alleviation: Different associations give philanthropic guide and help to those impacted by clashes and catastrophic events. This help is essential in the midst of emergency.

Training and Support: Bringing issues to light and instructing general society about continuous worldwide difficulties is fundamental. Promotion endeavors and grassroots drives can drive change and draw in networks in resolving these issues.

Supportable Works on: Empowering reasonable practices in enterprises, farming, and asset the executives is basic for tending to natural and food security challenges.

Discretion and Compromise: Conciliatory endeavors and compromise procedures are fundamental to tending to political flimsiness and clashes, as well as advancing harmony and compromise.

Chapter 7

Regulatory And Compliance Challenges

In the present globalized and interconnected world, associations face a large number of administrative and consistence challenges. These difficulties emerge from a perplexing trap of regulations, guidelines, and guidelines intended to guarantee moral direct, safeguard buyers, and keep up with the trustworthiness of different businesses. Exploring this administrative scene is in many cases a mind boggling and continuous fight, set apart by the two open doors and entanglements. In this article, we will investigate the administrative and consistence challenges that associations experience, the ramifications of resistance, and techniques for actually tending to them.

Understanding Administrative and Consistence Difficulties

Administrative and consistence challenges incorporate a large number of issues and are many times molded by the developing scene of administration, innovation, and strategic policies. A portion of the key difficulties include:

Intricacy of Guidelines: The sheer number and intricacy of guidelines are overwhelming. Associations should battle with a huge number of industry-explicit principles, natural guidelines, work regulations, information security regulations, and then some. Understanding and complying with these guidelines can be an unpredictable errand.

Globalization: As associations extend worldwide, they should consent to a different arrangement of public and worldwide guidelines. The distinctions in general sets of laws and administrative prerequisites across nations add a layer of intricacy to consistence endeavors.

Mechanical Headways: Fast mechanical progressions have led to new difficulties in information security, protection, and moral utilization of innovation. With the reception of arising innovations like computerized reasoning (artificial intelligence) and the Web of Things (IoT), associations should remain current with developing guidelines.

Network safety: The developing commonness of digital dangers and information breaks requires vigorous network safety measures to guarantee consistence with information security guidelines, like the Overall Information Assurance Guideline (GDPR) and the Medical coverage Conveyability and Responsibility Act (HIPAA).

Information Security: The insurance of individual information is a worldwide concern. Guidelines like GDPR in the European Association and the California Purchaser Security Act (CCPA) in the US expect associations to carry out measures to protect people's information.

Store network Intricacy: Worldwide stockpile chains are perplexing, including numerous partners, accomplices, and sellers. Guaranteeing consistence inside these perplexing stockpile chains is testing, especially in enterprises like assembling and retail.

Hostile to Illegal tax avoidance (AML) and Against Defilement Regulations: AML guidelines expect associations to forestall tax evasion exercises and consent to worldwide principles. Hostile to defilement regulations, like the U.S. Unfamiliar Degenerate Practices Act (FCPA) and the UK Pay off Act, address degenerate practices in deals.

Natural Guidelines: Organizations face a developing number of ecological guidelines pointed toward diminishing ozone depleting substance discharges, waste, and contamination. These guidelines expect associations to embrace eco-accommodating practices and advancements.

HR and Work Regulations: Business and work guidelines incorporate a scope of issues, including the lowest pay permitted by law, representative freedoms, segregation, and working environment wellbeing. Consistence with these regulations is fundamental for safeguarding representatives and keeping up with moral practices.

Monetary Revealing and Bookkeeping Norms: Consistence with monetary announcing and bookkeeping guidelines is basic for guaranteeing straightforwardness and forestalling monetary misrepresentation. Guidelines like the Sarbanes-Oxley Act (SOX) set rigid principles for monetary revelations.

Ramifications of Resistance

Neglecting to meet administrative and consistence necessities can have extreme ramifications for associations. A portion of the ramifications of resistance include:

Legitimate Outcomes: Resistance can bring about legitimate activities, including fines, punishments, and claims. Administrative bodies have the power to authorize these punishments, which can monetarily obliterate.

Reputational Harm: Resistance can discolor an association's standing, prompting the deficiency of client trust and certainty. A harmed standing can bring about diminished deals, piece of the pie, and benefit.

Functional Disturbance: Administrative infringement might prompt functional interruptions as associations should address consistence issues, which can be tedious and exorbitant.

Monetary Effect: The expense of consistence endeavors, punishments, and potential claims can monetarily affect associations, possibly influencing their capacity to put resources into development and advancement.

Information Breaks and Network safety Dangers: Resistance with information insurance guidelines can expand the gamble of information breaks and online protection dangers, possibly uncovering touchy client data and licensed innovation.

Store network Disturbance: Inability to conform to store network guidelines can upset tasks and result in challenges in obtaining materials or items from providers.

Loss of Market Access: now and again, rebelliousness can prompt associations being prohibited from specific business sectors, decreasing their worldwide reach and potential learning experiences.

Techniques for Tending to Administrative and Consistence Difficulties

Really tending to administrative and consistence challenges requires an essential methodology. Here are a few procedures associations can utilize to explore this perplexing scene:

Consistence The executives Frameworks: Carrying out consistence the board frameworks (CMS) can assist associations efficiently track and oversee consistence with important guidelines. These frameworks incorporate approaches, strategies, and innovation instruments to screen, report, and address consistence issues.

Normal Reviews and Appraisals: Direct customary reviews and evaluations of consistence endeavors to distinguish holes and areas of progress. Outer reviews by free specialists can give an objective viewpoint.

Legitimate and Administrative Specialists: Associations can profit from the aptitude of lawful and administrative experts who can give direction on understanding and complying with complex guidelines.

Preparing and Schooling: Put resources into preparing and training projects to guarantee workers comprehend the guidelines that apply to their jobs. This incorporates network safety preparing, morals preparing, and information assurance schooling.

Innovation Arrangements: Influence innovation answers for assist with consistence. These may incorporate information encryption, online protection programming, information the board devices, and consistence programming that computerizes processes.

Worldwide Consistence Groups: For associations with worldwide tasks, lay out worldwide consistence groups that can address locale explicit administrative necessities while keeping a brought together consistence methodology.

Outsider Gamble The board: Associations ought to survey and deal with the consistence of their outsider sellers and accomplices, as rebelliousness in the production network can affect the association's own consistence status.

Moral Culture: Develop a moral corporate culture that values consistence with guidelines and moral direct. Representative mindfulness and obligation to moral practices are basic.

Flexibility and Constant Observing: Remain versatile and consistently screen the administrative scene for changes and updates. Guidelines develop, and associations should advance with them.

The Job of Administrative Bodies

Administrative bodies assume a crucial part in upholding and forming consistence principles. They add to tending to administrative and consistence challenges by:

Strategy Improvement: Administrative bodies create and change guidelines to address current difficulties and issues in their separate areas.

Authorization: They screen consistence and implement guidelines through reviews, examinations, and punishments for rebelliousness.

Direction and Schooling: Administrative bodies give direction and instructive assets to help associations comprehend and meet consistence prerequisites.

Information Assortment: They accumulate information and experiences to evaluate the effect of guidelines and foster proof based guidelines.

Debate Goal: Administrative bodies frequently intercede questions connected with consistence, offering a stage for settling issues.

7.1Regulatory Evolution in Banking

The financial business is a foundation of any cutting edge economy, assuming a basic part in working with monetary development and monetary strength. To guarantee the viable working of this area, administrative structures have advanced altogether throughout the long term. The development of banking guidelines has been driven by different elements, including monetary emergencies, mechanical headways, and changes in market elements. This article digs into the verifiable improvement of banking guidelines, looking at key achievements and the elements that molded them. Furthermore, it investigates the contemporary administrative scene in banking and expects the likely future bearings of these guidelines.

Authentic Improvement of Banking Guidelines

Early Financial Guidelines

The starting points of banking guidelines can be followed back to antiquated civic establishments like Babylon and Old Rome. These early guidelines fundamentally centered around issues of credit, obligation, and financing costs. For instance, the Code of Hammurabi (1754 BC) included arrangements managing loaning and financing costs.

The Financial Demonstration of 1863

In the US, the Public Financial Demonstration of 1863 was a huge achievement in financial guideline. It laid out an arrangement of public banks and made a uniform cash. This undeniable the start of a more concentrated and organized administrative way to deal with banking.

The Central bank Framework

The Central bank Demonstration of 1913 laid out the Central bank Framework in the US, which filled in as a reaction to the continuous monetary frenzies of the late nineteenth and mid twentieth hundreds of years. This framework gave a national bank the power to manage and settle the country's monetary framework.

The Glass-Steagall Act

The Glass-Steagall Demonstration of 1933 is one more significant second in financial guideline. It isolated business banking from speculation banking, intending to forestall irreconcilable circumstances and lessen foundational gambles. This guideline stayed set up for a long time and was to some degree revoked in 1999.

Post-The Second Great War Period

In the post-The Second Great War period, the Bretton Woods Understanding laid out a proper conversion scale framework and prompted the making of the Global Financial Asset (IMF) and the World Bank. These organizations assumed a huge part in molding worldwide financial guidelines by giving monetary soundness and improvement help.

Monetary Liberation

During the last 50% of the twentieth 100 years, numerous nations, including the US and the Unified Realm, set out on a way of monetary liberation. This period saw the evacuation of different limitations on financial exercises, prompting more prominent development and contest. Nonetheless, it additionally added to the circumstances that prompted the 2008 monetary emergency.

The Basel Accords

The Basel Accords, which started with Basel I in 1988 and went on with Basel II in 2004, and Basel III in 2010, presented global financial guidelines. These arrangements zeroed in on capital sufficiency, risk the executives, and administrative oversight, assuming a critical part in working on the versatility of the worldwide financial framework.

Contemporary Financial Guidelines

Post-Worldwide Monetary Emergency Changes

The 2008 worldwide monetary emergency provoked a reassessment of banking guidelines around the world. State run administrations and administrative bodies carried out different changes to address the weaknesses uncovered by the emergency. Key changes incorporated the Dodd-Plain Money Road Change and Buyer Assurance Act in the US, which acquainted massive changes with monetary guideline and made the Customer Monetary Security Agency (CFPB).

Expanded Capital Necessities

One of the key changes following the monetary emergency was the expansion in capital prerequisites for banks. Basel III, for example, acquainted stricter capital principles with guarantee that banks held adequate cash-flow to retain misfortunes during times of monetary pressure. These capital necessities are intended to lessen the probability of bank disappointments and fundamental dangers.

Stress Testing

Stress testing turned into a basic part of banking guideline. It includes surveying a bank's capacity to endure unfavorable monetary circumstances. Controllers expect banks to go through normal pressure tests to guarantee they have sufficient capital and liquidity cushions to endure monetary shocks.

Liquidity Necessities

Controllers additionally acquainted liquidity necessities with guarantee that banks have an adequate number of fluid resources for meet momentary commitments. These prerequisites intend to forestall circumstances where a bank might not be able to meet its commitments because of an unexpected loss of financing.

Goal Systems

To resolve the issue of "too enormous to even think about falling flat," numerous nations created goal structures that frame the cycle for slowing down or recapitalizing bombing banks. These structures are planned to limit the effect on the more extensive monetary framework and safeguard citizens from bearing the expense of bailouts.

Buyer Insurance

Buyer security in banking turned into a need, with the foundation of organizations like the Customer Monetary Security Department in the US. These organizations work to guarantee that purchasers are dealt with decently by monetary establishments and approach clear, straightforward monetary items.

Future Ramifications of Banking Guidelines

Mechanical Advancement

The quick headway of innovation is reshaping the financial business. The rise of fintech and computerized banks has brought up issues about how conventional financial guidelines will adjust to this new scene. Controllers should find some kind of harmony between encouraging development and shielding monetary steadiness.

Network protection and Information Security

As the financial business turns out to be progressively computerized, network protection and information security will be basic worries. Future guidelines should address the insurance of client information and the avoidance of cyberattacks. This might include the execution of more rigid online protection guidelines and prerequisites.

Environment Hazard and Maintainability

The acknowledgment of environmental change as a foundational hazard to the monetary framework has prompted conversations about integrating environment risk into banking guidelines. Future guidelines might expect banks to evaluate and unveil their openness to environment related gambles, possibly prompting changes in loaning practices and venture choices.

Global Collaboration

The worldwide idea of the financial business requires global participation on guidelines. As banking guidelines keep on advancing, orchestrating principles across boundaries will be fundamental to guarantee predictable and compelling oversight of worldwide banks.

Development of Installment Frameworks

The ascent of computerized monetary standards, like cryptographic forms of money and national bank advanced monetary standards (CBDCs), presents administrative difficulties and potential open doors. Controllers should foster systems to address the dangers and advantages related with these new types of cash.

Monetary Incorporation

Controllers are progressively zeroing in on monetary consideration, trying to guarantee that underserved populaces approach banking administrations. Future guidelines might expect banks to put forth attempts to reach unbanked and underbanked networks.

Enormous Tech in Banking

The passage of huge tech organizations into the monetary administrations area, frequently alluded to as "Large TechFin," presents remarkable difficulties to banking guidelines. Controllers should consider how to apply customary financial guidelines to these tech goliaths and forestall expected maltreatments of market power.

7.2AML and KYC Compliance

Against Tax evasion (AML) and Know Your Client (KYC) consistence are fundamental mainstays of the worldwide monetary framework. During a time set apart by expanding monetary intricacy and complexity, these guidelines assume a basic part in forestalling unlawful monetary exercises, keeping up with the trustworthiness of the monetary area, and guaranteeing the security of monetary establishments and their clients. This article investigates the meaning of AML and KYC consistence, their goals, key parts, and the difficulties they present in the present monetary scene.

The Meaning of AML and KYC Consistence

AML Consistence

Against Tax evasion (AML) guidelines are intended to forestall and recognize the criminal behavior of illegal tax avoidance, which includes disguising the beginnings of unlawfully gotten assets by causing them to seem authentic. Illegal tax avoidance represents a critical danger to the monetary framework, as it can work with different wrongdoings, including drug dealing, psychological oppression supporting, and tax avoidance. AML consistence shields the monetary business by following and revealing dubious monetary exchanges to the proper specialists.

KYC Consistence

Know Your Client (KYC) consistence is a significant part of AML guidelines. KYC systems require monetary establishments to check the personality of their clients and survey their gamble factors. Thusly, they can guarantee that their clients are genuine and not engaged with criminal operations. KYC consistence isn't just fundamental for forestalling tax evasion yet additionally for identifying and forestalling extortion, data fraud, and other monetary violations.

Goals of AML and KYC Consistence

The essential goals of AML and KYC consistence are as per the following:

Avoidance of Tax evasion: AML guidelines mean to forestall the utilization of the monetary framework for illegal tax avoidance exercises. By following and announcing dubious exchanges, monetary establishments help specialists explore and indict tax criminals.

Recognition and Detailing of Dubious Exercises: Monetary foundations should lay out methodology to distinguish and report any uncommon or dubious exercises that might be demonstrative of tax evasion or fear monger funding.

Client An expected level of effort: KYC consistence guarantees that monetary foundations have an exhaustive comprehension of their clients, their monetary exercises, and their gamble profiles. This information empowers foundations to recognize any irregularities or dubious way of behaving.

Improved Security: AML and KYC estimates upgrade the general security of the monetary framework, decreasing the dangers related with monetary wrongdoings and safeguarding the standing of monetary foundations.

Key Parts of AML and KYC Consistence

Client ID: The underpinning of KYC consistence is the check of client characters. This cycle includes gathering data like name, address, date of birth, and official recognizable proof reports.

Risk Evaluation: Monetary foundations direct gamble appraisals to arrange their clients into low, medium, or high-risk gatherings. This assists them with fitting their reasonable level of effort methodology appropriately.

Progressing Checking: Nonstop observing of client records and exchanges is urgent. Any huge deviations from expected conduct ought to be completely examined.

Dubious Action Detailing: Monetary establishments are expected to report any dubious exchanges to administrative specialists. Announcing edges and methodology fluctuate by locale.

AML/KYC Preparing: Staff ought to get customary preparation to remain refreshed on AML and KYC guidelines, guaranteeing that they can really recognize and report dubious exercises.

Record-Keeping: Exact and coordinated record-keeping is fundamental for consistence. Establishments should hold records of client data, exchanges, and dubious action reports for a predefined period.

Challenges in AML and KYC Consistence

Advancing Monetary Violations: Monetary lawbreakers constantly adjust to new guidelines and innovation. They track down creative ways of laundering cash and take advantage of weaknesses in the framework, making it provoking for establishments to keep up.

Administrative Intricacy: The administrative scene can be intricate and may differ altogether across purviews. Global monetary organizations should explore different AML and KYC necessities, prompting consistence challenges.

Client Experience: Finding some kind of harmony between vigorous consistence measures and a smooth client experience is a consistent test. Extensive and nosy KYC cycles can stop likely clients.

Information The executives: Dealing with huge volumes of client information and exchange records can be asset concentrated and may require critical interests in information the board and network safety.

Misleading Up-sides: AML programming frequently creates various bogus up-sides, which require manual survey. This can bring about an excess and possibly permit real dubious exchanges to slip by everyone's notice.

Asset Limitations: More modest monetary organizations might confront asset requirements in carrying out far reaching AML and KYC consistence programs, making them more powerless against administrative examination and monetary violations.

Future Patterns and Developments

As the monetary scene develops, so do AML and KYC consistence strategies. A few arising patterns and developments in the field include:

Man-made brainpower (simulated intelligence) and AI: artificial intelligence and AI are being utilized to upgrade AML and KYC processes by working on the precision of exchange checking and diminishing bogus up-sides.

Blockchain and Conveyed Record Innovation: These advancements offer straightforward and unchanging record-keeping, which can improve on KYC cycles and upgrade the security of client information.

Administrative Innovation (RegTech): RegTech arrangements are assisting monetary foundations with mechanizing consistence processes, making it simpler to keep awake to date with evolving guidelines.

Joint effort and Data Sharing: Cooperation among monetary organizations and administrative specialists can help in the battle against monetary wrongdoings by sharing data and best practices.

Concentrated KYC Utilities: A few districts are investigating the foundation of unified data sets that would store KYC data for numerous monetary organizations, lessening overt repetitiveness and improving effectiveness.

7.3PSD2 and Open Banking

The monetary business is going through a significant change, driven by progressions in innovation, developing client assumptions, and administrative drives. Two vital parts of this change are the Installment Administrations Mandate 2 (PSD2) and the idea of Open Banking. These drives are reshaping the manner in which banking works, advancing rivalry, development, and client strengthening while at the same time underscoring information security and protection. This article investigates the crucial standards of PSD2 and Open Banking, their effects on the monetary area, and the open doors and difficulties they present.

Figuring out PSD2

The Installment Administrations Mandate (PSD): The Installment Administrations Order is an European Association mandate that manages installment administrations and installment specialist co-ops inside the European Monetary Region (EEA). The underlying PSD was taken on in 2007, and its essential objective was to make a solitary market for installments in the EU, normalizing installment frameworks and improving rivalry.

PSD2: Expanding upon the outcome of the first PSD, PSD2 was presented in 2015 and became powerful in January 2018. PSD2 addresses a critical development of the administrative structure, presenting new prerequisites and valuable open doors for installment administrations and banking.

Key Components of PSD2

Admittance to Records (XS2A): PSD2 orders that banks give outsider suppliers (TPPs), with the client's assent, admittance to their records and exchange information. This entrance means to cultivate advancement and contest by empowering the production of new installment and banking administrations.

Solid Client Confirmation (SCA): To upgrade security, PSD2 presents SCA, which requires multifaceted validation for electronic installment exchanges. This adds an additional layer of insurance for customers when they start electronic exchanges.

Installment Inception Specialist organizations (PISPs) and Record Data Specialist organizations (AISPs): PISPs can start installments straightforwardly from the client's ledger, while AISPs give amassed monetary data from different records. These jobs are available to approved TPPs.

Administrative Specialized Norms (RTS): The European Financial Power (EBA) laid out RTS to guarantee predictable use of PSD2 across the EU. These principles characterize explicit necessities for verification, approval, and functional cycles.

Effects of PSD2

Improved Rivalry: PSD2 has made the ways for expanded contest in the monetary area. New participants, for example, fintech organizations and outsider suppliers, can offer imaginative installment and banking administrations that were recently held for conventional banks.

Purchaser Strengthening: PSD2 places buyers in charge of their monetary information. They have the power to allow and renounce admittance to their monetary data, giving more noteworthy straightforwardness and command over their funds.

Development: The mandate has prodded advancement in the monetary business. Fintech organizations are creating arrangements that influence admittance to financial balances, bringing about better installment choices, individual budget the executives, and that's only the tip of the iceberg.

Security: SCA, a critical part of PSD2, improves the security of electronic installment exchanges. It makes it essentially more moving for fraudsters to acquire unapproved admittance to accounts.

Grasping Open Banking

Open Banking is a more extensive idea that reaches out past the EU and includes comparative standards to PSD2, with a worldwide point of view. Open Financial looks to engage buyers by empowering them to share their monetary information safely with confided in outsiders. It empowers the advancement of inventive administrations that can work on monetary administration, smooth out installments, and give customized arrangements.

Key Components of Open Banking

APIs (Application Programming Connection points): Open Financial depends on APIs that permit outsider designers to get to monetary information and administrations in a normalized and secure way. APIs work with information trade between monetary organizations and outsiders.

Information Sharing Assent: Purchasers have the position to concede assent for imparting their monetary information to approved outsiders. They can oversee and disavow authorizations depending on the situation.

Rivalry and Advancement: Open Financial encourages contest and development by empowering new participants to offer monetary administrations and items. Customary banks are urged to adjust and advance to keep up with their market positions.

Security and Protection: Information security and security are fundamental in Open Banking. Thorough safety efforts are set up to defend delicate monetary data. The Overall Information Assurance Guideline (GDPR) in the EU and comparable guidelines universally are essential to information security.

Effects of Open Banking

Shopper Driven Arrangements: Open Financial places customers steering the ship, permitting them to get to many administrations and contrast contributions with track down arrangements that best address their issues.

Fintech Development: Fintech organizations and new businesses have benefited from Open Banking to present creative items and administrations. These incorporate individual accounting the executives applications, distributed installment stages, and that's only the tip of the iceberg.

Worked on Monetary Administration: Open Banking furnishes customers with an extensive perspective on their monetary data across numerous establishments. This empowers better monetary preparation, planning, and speculation choices.

Market Contest: Customary banks face expanded rivalry from fintech firms and tech monsters. To stay cutthroat, they should upgrade their computerized contributions and client encounters.

Open doors and Difficulties

Open doors:

Development: PSD2 and Open Banking have opened a rush of development in the monetary area, bringing about new items and administrations that benefit buyers.

Monetary Incorporation: Open Banking can add to monetary consideration by making monetary administrations more available and reasonable for underserved populaces.

Client Driven Banking: These drives place buyers at the middle, empowering them to get to customized, easy to use monetary administrations.

Challenges:

Security Concerns: The expanded admittance to monetary information and records requires powerful safety efforts to forestall information breaks and extortion.

Administrative Consistence: Monetary organizations should explore complex administrative systems to guarantee they are consistent with PSD2 and Open Financial guidelines.

Information Security: The sharing of individual monetary information raises worries about information protection and insurance, focusing on adherence to information assurance regulations.

Joining: Carrying out Open Banking and following PSD2 can be actually difficult and expensive for monetary organizations, especially more modest players.

7.4The Future of Banking Regulations

The eventual fate of banking guidelines is ready at the crossing point of various unique powers, including mechanical development, monetary intricacy, and advancing worldwide difficulties. As the monetary area goes through quick change, administrative structures should adjust to guarantee monetary solidness, shopper insurance, and the uprightness of the financial framework. This article investigates the vital patterns and contemplations forming the eventual fate of banking guidelines.

Advanced Change and Mechanical Development:

The approach of fintech, blockchain, man-made reasoning, and advanced banking is changing the monetary area. These advancements achieve new open doors and difficulties for controllers.

1. **Regtech:** Administrative innovation (Regtech) is assuming a urgent part in assisting monetary establishments and controllers with staying up with mechanical progressions. Regtech arrangements use man-made intelligence and information examination to computerize consistence processes, upgrade risk the board, and recognize monetary violations all the more productively.
2. **Online protection:** With expanded digitalization, network safety is a top concern. Administrative organizations are zeroing in on information security and the avoidance of digital dangers. Future guidelines will probably incorporate stricter online protection norms and prerequisites.

Monetary Consideration and Buyer Assurance:

The drive for monetary consideration and upgraded shopper insurance stays a vital need for controllers around the world.

1. **Open Banking:** Drives like PSD2 and Open Banking empower purchasers to get to a more extensive scope of administrations, and this pattern is supposed to proceed. Controllers should guarantee that such administrations don't think twice about protection or security.
2. **Computerized Monetary standards and National Bank Computerized Monetary standards (CBDCs):** The ascent of computerized monetary standards, including cryptographic forms of money and CBDCs, will require the improvement of guidelines that find some kind of harmony between cultivating development and guaranteeing strength and security.

Environmental Change and Supportability:

Environmental change is progressively being perceived as a foundational hazard to the monetary framework. Subsequently, administrative structures are probably going to consolidate environment risk contemplations.

1. **Environment Divulgence:** Guidelines might require monetary foundations to survey and uncover their openness to environment related gambles. This could impact loaning rehearses, venture choices, and hazard evaluations.
2. **Green Money:** Administrative help for green money, which advances interests in earth economical undertakings, is supposed to develop. Manageable money guidelines will be a key center region.

Worldwide Collaboration and Harmonization:

Banking is an intrinsically worldwide industry, and the requirement for global collaboration on guidelines has never been more prominent.

1. **Basel System:** The Basel Board of trustees on Financial Oversight's structure keeps on assuming a fundamental part in worldwide financial guidelines. Future Basel Accords might address developing dangers and difficulties in the financial business.
2. **Information Sharing and Cooperation:** Controllers across various districts are probably going to team up on information sharing to battle illegal tax avoidance, monetary violations, and network safety dangers all the more really.

Huge Tech in Banking:

Huge tech organizations, including any semblance of Google, Amazon, Facebook, and Apple, are progressively entering the monetary administrations area, a pattern known as "Large TechFin."

1. **Rivalry and Guideline:** Controllers should consider how to apply conventional financial standards to these tech goliaths and forestall possible maltreatments of market power. Offsetting development and rivalry with purchaser insurance will be foremost.

Worldwide Monetary Emergencies and Fundamental Gamble:
Recollections of the 2008 monetary emergency and worries about future foundational gambles with keep on shaping administrative reasoning.

1. **Goal Systems:** To address the "too enormous to even consider fizzling" issue, numerous nations have created goal structures that frame the cycle for slowing down or recapitalizing bombing banks. These structures plan to safeguard the more extensive monetary framework and forestall citizen financed bailouts.
2. **Stress Testing:** Stress testing will stay a basic part of banking guideline. Controllers will keep on evaluating a bank's capacity to endure monetary shocks, guaranteeing they have adequate capital and liquidity cradles.

Administrative Revealing and Straightforwardness:
Administrative announcing is turning out to be progressively complex, with controllers requesting additional granular information from monetary establishments.

1. **Ongoing Announcing:** Controllers are investigating continuous information answering to recognize and resolve issues before they grow into emergencies.
2. **Straightforwardness:** Improved straightforwardness in monetary detailing will stay a point of convergence, guaranteeing that purchasers and partners approach precise and forward-thinking data.

Chapter 8

The Rise Of Neobanks

As of late, a critical change has been unfurling in the monetary business, driven by another type of monetary establishments known as neobanks. These computerized just, branchless banks are rethinking the manner in which people and organizations deal with their funds. The ascent of neobanks is a demonstration of the developing interest for more helpful, client driven, and mechanically progressed financial administrations. This article dives into the starting points, development, and effect of neobanks on the customary financial scene.

Grasping Neobanks

Beginnings of Neobanks:

Neobanks, frequently alluded to as computerized banks, challenger banks, or application based banks, arose during the 2010s as a reaction to the weaknesses of customary banks. These monetary new companies tried to use innovation to address client trouble spots, like bulky record the board, high expenses, and absence of straightforwardness.

Key Qualities:

Neobanks share a few central traits:

1. **Advanced As it were:** Neobanks work exclusively through computerized channels, killing the requirement for physical branches.
2. **Client Driven:** These banks focus on client experience, offering easy to understand portable applications, fast onboarding, and responsive client service.
3. **Imaginative Innovation:** Neobanks influence state of the art innovation, including computerized reasoning, enormous information examination, and distributed computing, to improve their administrations.
4. **Straightforward Estimating:** Neobanks commonly have direct expense structures, offering cutthroat or no-charge accounts and straightforward unfamiliar trade rates.

5. **Accomplice Environments:** Numerous neobanks structure organizations with other fintech organizations to offer a more extensive scope of administrations, like venture items and protection.

The Development of Neobanks

Worldwide Development:

The progress of neobanks was at first moved in districts like Europe and the US. European neobanks, for example, N26 and Revolut, acquired conspicuousness by offering consistent cross-line administrations. They set a worldwide precedent, prompting the development of neobanks in Asia, Australia, and South America.

Different Contributions:

Neobanks have extended past fundamental conditional administrations. They presently offer a wide cluster of monetary items, including investment accounts, venture portfolios, and, surprisingly, private company banking arrangements.

Subsidizing and Valuations:

Neobanks have drawn in significant ventures, major areas of strength for reflecting trust in their development potential. Their valuations have flooded, stamping them as imposing players in the monetary area.

Effect of Neobanks

Expanded Rivalry:

Neobanks have disturbed the customary financial scene by offering more light-footed, client centered administrations. This has prodded expanded contest in the area, driving laid out banks to upgrade their computerized contributions and further develop client encounters.

Shopper Strengthening:

Neobanks engage shoppers by giving them more prominent command over their funds, improved monetary perceivability, and admittance to inventive instruments for saving, financial planning, and planning.

Diminished Expenses and Charges:

The expense construction of neobanks is many times better for buyers, as they commonly offer low or no-charge accounts and cutthroat unfamiliar trade rates. This has placed tension on conventional banks to reexamine their charge structures.

Monetary Consideration:

Neobanks are addressing monetary consideration by giving financial administrations to underbanked and unbanked people, as they frequently have lower passage obstructions and more available record opening cycles.

Associations and Biological systems:

Neobanks frequently team up with fintech organizations and outsider suppliers to extend their item contributions. These associations make incorporated monetary environments that take care of different client needs.

Challenges Looked by Neobanks

Administrative Consistence:

Neobanks should explore complex administrative scenes, which differ from one country to another. Meeting the tough administrative necessities for monetary organizations can challenge.

Client Trust:

Acquiring and keeping up with client trust is fundamental, as computerized just banks need actual branches. Any network protection break or information hole could dissolve client certainty.

Benefit:

In spite of huge development, numerous neobanks are not yet productive. They frequently lose money because of weighty interests in innovation, client obtaining, and consistence.

Versatility:

Accomplishing versatility is really difficult for neobanks. As their client base develops, they should guarantee that their innovation foundation can uphold the expanded volume of exchanges and client connections.

Administrative Examination:

Controllers overall are keeping a nearby watch on the neobanking area. As neobanks keep on offering a more extensive cluster of monetary administrations, controllers might force more rigid necessities to guarantee purchaser insurance and monetary dependability.

The Eventual fate of Neobanks

Combination and Development:

The neobanking area is probably going to observe combination as bigger players gain more modest ones. As the business develops, neobanks should zero in on becoming productive and accomplishing economical development.

Administrative Development:

Administrative changes are supposed to shape the future of neobanks. Controllers will probably adjust to the advanced financial scene, forcing stricter norms to guarantee client assurance, information security, and monetary strength.

Worldwide Development:

Neobanks will keep on growing internationally, arriving at new business sectors and expanding their item contributions to draw in a more extensive client base.

Advancement and Separation:

Neobanks will keep up with their attention on advancement to separate themselves from customary banks. We can hope to see the proceeded with advancement of state of the art monetary items and administrations.

Associations and Biological systems:

Neobanks will produce more organizations with fintech organizations and other specialist co-ops, making sweeping monetary environments that take care of an extensive variety of client needs.

8.1What are Neobanks?

As of late, a troublesome power has arisen in the realm of banking, testing conventional monetary foundations and changing the manner in which we deal with our cash. These disruptors, known as neobanks, are rethinking the financial scene with a new and inventive methodology. This article dives into the idea of neobanks, what they are, the means by which they vary from customary banks, and the effect they are having on the monetary business.

What Are Neobanks?

Neobanks, frequently alluded to as computerized banks, challenger banks, or application based banks, are another variety of monetary establishments that deal banking administrations only through advanced channels.

Not at all like customary keeps money with physical branches, neobanks work completely web based, depending on web and portable applications to give a scope of monetary administrations, including bank accounts, installments, credits, and the sky is the limit from there.

Key Attributes of Neobanks

Advanced Just Presence:

Neobanks don't have actual branch areas. Their whole financial activity, from client onboarding to exchange handling, is directed through computerized stages, for example, portable applications and web interfaces.

Client Driven Approach:

Client experience is at the center of neobanks' way of thinking. They focus on easy to understand interfaces, fast onboarding processes, and responsive client assistance. This attention on client needs separates them from numerous conventional banks.

Inventive Innovation:

Neobanks influence state of the art innovation to smooth out financial cycles. Computerized reasoning (artificial intelligence), huge information investigation, and distributed computing are normally used to improve their administrations. These innovations permit neobanks to offer customized monetary arrangements and enhance client collaborations.

Straightforward Valuing:

Neobanks frequently take on direct and straightforward expense structures. They mean to kill stowed away accuses and give clients of lucidity with respect to account upkeep charges, exchange expenses, and unfamiliar trade rates.

Accomplice Biological systems:

Numerous neobanks lay out organizations with other fintech organizations and specialist co-ops to widen their item contributions. These joint efforts permit them to give a more far reaching set-up of monetary administrations, including protection, ventures, and individual budget the board instruments.

Recognizing Neobanks from Customary Banks

Branchless Activities:

The most apparent contrast is that neobanks don't keep up with actual branches. Clients access their records, make exchanges, and look for help through advanced stages, while customary banks commonly depend on branch organizations.

Lower Overheads:

Neobanks work with essentially lower above costs contrasted with conventional banks, which should keep up with actual areas and a bigger labor force. This cost productivity frequently converts into more cutthroat expense designs and bank account loan fees for neobank clients.

Fast Onboarding:

Neobanks focus on easy to understand and proficient onboarding processes. Clients can open records in no time flat, frequently with a basic photograph of ID and a couple of taps on a portable application. Conventional banks might require greater documentation and in-person visits.

Imaginative Administrations:

Neobanks offer many creative monetary administrations, for example, virtual charge cards, gather together reserve funds, distributed installments, and the sky is the limit from there. They will generally be more deft and receptive to client requests with regards to presenting new elements.

Worldwide Availability:

Numerous neobanks mean to serve a worldwide crowd. With highlights like no-expense global exchanges and serious unfamiliar trade rates, they take special care of people and organizations with cross-line monetary requirements. Conventional banks frequently have more restricted global administrations.

The Development and Effect of Neobanks

Worldwide Development:

Neobanks at first acquired unmistakable quality in districts like Europe, where organizations, for example, N26 and Revolut drove the charge. This achievement set a worldwide precedent, prompting the development of neobanks in Asia, Australia, South America, and North America.

Different Contributions:

After some time, neobanks have extended their contributions past essential value-based administrations. Many presently give investment accounts, speculation portfolios, credit items, and, surprisingly, private company banking arrangements, tending to a more extensive scope of monetary necessities.

Financing and Valuations:

Neobanks have drawn in huge ventures, serious areas of strength for highlighting trust in their development potential. This certainty is clear in the flood in valuations for the majority neobank new businesses, situating them as considerable players in the monetary business.

Expanded Contest:

The outcome of neobanks has disturbed the conventional financial scene, encouraging expanded rivalry. Laid out banks are currently constrained to upgrade their computerized contributions, further develop client encounters, and return to their expense designs to stay serious.

Client Strengthening:

Neobanks enable purchasers by giving them more noteworthy command over their funds. Clients can get to their records, view exchanges, put forth investment funds objectives, and oversee spending plans through easy to use versatile applications. This improved monetary perceivability has turned into a foundation of neobank administrations.

Diminished Expenses and Charges:

Neobanks frequently offer better expense structures for clients. Numerous neobanks give no-charge accounts or cutthroat unfamiliar trade rates, making tension on conventional banks to rethink their expense structures.

Monetary Consideration

Neobanks add to monetary consideration by serving underbanked and unbanked people. Their streamlined onboarding processes and available record the executives make it more straightforward for individuals to get to fundamental financial administrations.

Challenges Looked by Neobanks

While neobanks have taken critical steps in the monetary business, they likewise experience a few difficulties:

Administrative Consistence:

Neobanks should explore complex administrative scenes. They should comply with rigid monetary guidelines that shift from one country to another, making consistence a huge test.

Client Trust:

Acquiring and keeping up with client trust is pivotal for neobanks. Since they need actual branches, any online protection breaks or information holes could disintegrate client certainty and notoriety.

Productivity:

In spite of their development, numerous neobanks are not yet beneficial. They lose money because of interests in innovation, client obtaining, and administrative consistence. Accomplishing benefit while proceeding to improve stays a huge test.

Adaptability:

As neobanks draw in a bigger client base, they should guarantee that their innovation framework can uphold the expanded volume of exchanges and client collaborations. Versatility stays a perplexing issue for neobanks.

Administrative Examination:

Controllers overall are watching out for the neobanking area. As neobanks offer a more extensive cluster of monetary administrations, controllers might force more rigid necessities to guarantee shopper security and monetary solidness.

The Fate of Neobanks

Combination and Development:

The neobanking area is supposed to see union as bigger players gain more modest ones. As the business develops, neobanks should zero in on becoming productive and accomplishing practical development.

Administrative Advancement:

Administrative changes will shape the future of neobanks. Controllers will adjust to the computerized financial scene, possibly forcing stricter norms to guarantee client security, information protection, and monetary dependability.

Worldwide Development:

Neobanks will keep on growing universally, arriving at new business sectors and differentiating their item contributions to draw in a more extensive client base.

Advancement and Separation:

Neobanks will keep up with their attention on development to separate themselves from conventional banks. Anticipate the proceeded with advancement of state of the art monetary items and administrations.

Organizations and Environments:

Neobanks will produce more organizations with fintech organizations and other specialist co-ops, making extensive monetary biological systems that take care of an extensive variety of client needs.

8.2Features and Advantages

In an undeniably computerized and interconnected world, current monetary administrations have developed to offer a wide cluster of elements and benefits that take care of the different necessities of purchasers, organizations, and the more extensive economy. These administrations influence state of the art innovation and inventive ways to deal with upgrade monetary administration, installments, speculations, and that's just the beginning. This article investigates the critical highlights and benefits of present day monetary administrations, revealing insight into the manners in which they engage people and associations the same.

Elements of Present day Monetary Administrations

Computerized Openness:

Present day monetary administrations are open through different computerized channels, including web stages and versatile applications. This openness permits clients to deal with their funds, make exchanges, and access administrations from basically anyplace, whenever.

Easy to understand Connection points:

These administrations focus on client experience with natural and easy to use interfaces. Improved on account the executives, smoothed out exchange processes, and direct route make it simple for clients to deal with their monetary issues.

Safety efforts:

High level security highlights, for example, multifaceted verification, encryption, and biometrics, guarantee that client information and exchanges are protected against unapproved access and digital dangers.

Inventive Installment Strategies:

Current monetary administrations offer creative installment techniques, including versatile wallets, shared (P2P) installments, and computerized cards. These techniques give comfort and adaptability to making exchanges.

Individual accounting The executives Apparatuses:

Numerous cutting edge administrations incorporate devices for planning, cost following, and monetary objective setting. These highlights assist clients with overseeing their funds and pursue informed choices.

Speculation Arrangements:

Robo-counselors, trade exchanged reserves (ETFs), and online financier administrations are ordinarily coordinated into present day monetary stages. These devices empower clients to put resources into stocks, bonds, and different resources effortlessly.

Global Administrations:

Current monetary administrations frequently support cross-line exchanges, offering cutthroat unfamiliar trade rates and worldwide record access. This takes special care of the requirements of clients with worldwide monetary interests.

Account Collection:

A few administrations permit clients to total numerous monetary records from various foundations, giving a concentrated perspective on their monetary portfolio and exchanges.

Benefits of Current Monetary Administrations

Comfort:

The computerized openness of present day monetary administrations makes overseeing funds and going through with exchanges more helpful than any time in recent memory. Clients can check account adjusts, make installments, and move assets from the solace of their own homes or while in a hurry.

Cost Reserve funds:

Numerous advanced administrations offer low or no-charge accounts, disposing of the requirement for exorbitant financial expenses. This cost-viability is especially beneficial for people and independent ventures.

Availability for the Unbanked and Underbanked:

Present day monetary administrations are instrumental in advancing monetary consideration. They offer improved on account opening cycles and administrations to people who might not have approached conventional banking.

Monetary Strengthening:

Individual accounting the board apparatuses, such as planning and cost following elements, enable clients to assume command over their monetary prosperity. They give bits of knowledge into ways of managing money, assisting clients with settling on informed choices.

Worldwide Exchanges:

Clients with global monetary interests benefit from serious unfamiliar trade rates and admittance to administrations that help cross-line exchanges. This can set aside cash and improve on global monetary connections.

Different Speculation Potential open doors:

The accessibility of speculation arrangements in current monetary administrations permits people to put resources into a differentiated arrangement of resources, possibly upgrading their monetary development and riches.

Upgraded Security:

Present day monetary administrations treat network safety in a serious way, utilizing progressed security elements to safeguard client information and exchanges. Clients can trust these administrations to defend their monetary data.

Thorough Biological systems:

Numerous cutting edge monetary administrations offer incorporated biological systems that give many monetary items and administrations. Clients can get to all that from banking and contributing to protection and retirement arranging inside a solitary stage.

Adaptability:

These administrations take care of clients with fluctuating monetary requirements. From fundamental banking to cutting edge venture arrangements, current monetary administrations offer adaptable choices that adjust to individual necessities.

Straightforwardness and Control:

Current monetary administrations offer clients more prominent straightforwardness in their monetary dealings. They can screen exchanges, put forth monetary objectives, and have constant perceivability into their records, giving a feeling of control and inner serenity.

Difficulties and Contemplations

While present day monetary administrations offer various benefits, they additionally accompany difficulties and contemplations:

Network safety Dangers:

As advanced stages, current monetary administrations are defenseless to online protection dangers. Clients should be cautious about safeguarding their login accreditations and individual data.

Administrative Consistence:

Guaranteeing consistence with monetary guidelines is fundamental for present day specialist co-ops. Administrative changes might affect administration contributions and client experience.

Information Protection:

Clients should believe that their own and monetary information is taken care of safely and secretly. Specialist co-ops should comply with information insurance regulations and strategies.

Market Immersion:

The rising number of computerized monetary specialist co-ops has prompted a serious market. Clients might have to research to pick the administrations that best address their issues.

Venture Dangers:

While current administrations offer speculation open doors, clients should know about the dangers related with putting resources into monetary business sectors.

8.3Disrupting Traditional Banking

The universe of customary banking, when portrayed by respected organizations and physical branches, is going through a huge change. This change is being driven by the ascent of fintech organizations and neobanks, which are upsetting the financial area by offering imaginative, client driven, and innovatively progressed monetary administrations. This article investigates the manners by which fintech and neobanks are testing conventional financial models and reshaping the monetary business.

Fintech: The Driving force of Disturbance

Fintech, a portmanteau of "monetary innovation," addresses a great many organizations and advancements that influence development to offer monetary types of assistance. These advancements envelop portable installments, shared loaning, blockchain, computerized wallets, robo-counselors, and that's just the beginning. Fintech organizations have quickly acquired noticeable quality for the accompanying reasons:

Inventive Items and Administrations: Fintech firms offer novel answers for longstanding financial difficulties. They have presented versatile installment applications like Square and Venmo, empowering speedy, advantageous, and minimal expense distributed exchanges.

Computerized Loaning: Online moneylenders, for example, LendingClub and Succeed have changed the loaning scene by improving on the getting system and diminishing the time it takes to get a credit. This has been particularly valuable for independent ventures and people.

Blockchain and Digital currency: Fintech has promoted the idea of blockchain and cryptographic forms of money like Bitcoin. Blockchain innovation is being investigated for its capability to further develop straightforwardness, security, and productivity in monetary exchanges.

Robo-Consultants: Fintech firms have presented mechanized speculation stages, known as robo-counselors, that offer calculation driven portfolio the board administrations. These stages give minimal expense speculation the board to retail financial backers.

Open Banking: Open banking, worked with by fintech organizations, empowers clients to share their monetary information safely with approved outsider suppliers. This enables buyers to get to a more extensive scope of administrations and better deal with their funds.

Neobanks: Branchless and Client Driven

Neobanks, or computerized banks, address a subset of fintech organizations that work solely on the web and don't have actual branch areas. These banks have acquired conspicuousness for the accompanying reasons:

Client Driven Approach: Neobanks focus on client experience by offering easy to understand versatile applications, fast onboarding, and responsive client assistance. This attention on client needs separates them from numerous customary banks.

Straightforwardness: Neobanks regularly have direct expense structures, offering cutthroat or no-charge accounts and straightforward unfamiliar trade rates. This straightforwardness assists clients with keeping away from stowed away charges.

Inventive Innovation: Utilizing state of the art innovation, including man-made consciousness, enormous information investigation, and distributed computing, neobanks can give customized monetary arrangements and advance client collaborations.

Security: Neobanks utilize progressed safety efforts, like solid encryption, multifaceted confirmation, and biometrics, to safeguard client information and exchanges.

Worldwide Openness: Numerous neobanks offer serious unfamiliar trade rates and backing cross-line exchanges, making them alluring to clients with global monetary interests.

Testing Customary Financial Models

Fintech and neobanks are upsetting customary financial models in more ways than one:

Computerized Just Presence: Not at all like conventional banks that keep up with physical branches, fintech organizations and neobanks work only through advanced channels. This wipes out the requirement for costly actual areas and takes into account cost reserve funds.

Lower Overheads: Conventional banks cause critical above costs related with keeping up with branches and a bigger labor force. Conversely, fintech organizations and neobanks work with lower overheads, empowering them to offer more aggressive expense designs and bank account loan fees.

Speedy Onboarding: Fintech organizations and neobanks focus on easy to understand and proficient onboarding processes. Clients can open records rapidly, frequently with a straightforward photograph of recognizable proof and a couple of taps on a versatile application. Customary banks might require greater documentation and in-person visits.

Inventive Administrations: Fintech organizations and neobanks offer creative monetary administrations, for example, virtual check cards, gather together reserve funds, shared installments, and computerized speculation choices. Customary banks might take more time to embrace such developments because of their laid out frameworks.

Worldwide Exchanges: Fintech organizations and neobanks frequently support cross-line exchanges, offering cutthroat unfamiliar trade rates and global record access. This takes special care of the necessities of clients with worldwide monetary interests, a portion that conventional banks may not act as successfully.

Extensive Environments: Numerous fintech organizations and neobanks give incorporated monetary biological systems that offer a large number of monetary items and administrations. This comprehensive methodology permits clients to get to banking, money management, protection, and other monetary administrations inside a solitary stage.

Monetary Consideration: Fintech organizations and neobanks have taken huge steps in advancing monetary incorporation. Their improved onboarding processes and open record the board make it simpler for individuals who were already underserved by conventional banks to get to fundamental monetary administrations.

Difficulties and Contemplations

While fintech and neobanks are disturbing conventional financial models and offering various benefits, they additionally face difficulties:

Administrative Consistence: Fintech organizations and neobanks should explore complex and advancing administrative scenes. Adherence to rigid monetary guidelines is fundamental to guarantee consistence and stay away from legitimate difficulties.

Information Protection: Clients should believe that their own and monetary information is dealt with safely and secretly. Specialist organizations should comply with information assurance regulations and arrangements.

Network safety Dangers: As computerized stages, fintech organizations and neobanks are defenseless to online protection dangers. They should constantly put resources into safety efforts to safeguard client information and exchanges.

Market Contest: The rising number of fintech and neobank suppliers has prompted a cutthroat market. Clients might have to research and contrast administrations with pick the ones that best address their issues.

Venture Dangers: While fintech organizations and neobanks offer speculation open doors, clients should know about the dangers related with putting resources into monetary business sectors.

8.4The Global Landscape

The fintech and neobanking insurgency significantly affects the worldwide monetary scene. As computerized innovation keeps on progressing, new monetary administrations suppliers are testing conventional financial models and offering imaginative, client driven arrangements. This article investigates the worldwide scene of fintech and neobanking, inspecting their fast development, market patterns, territorial contrasts, and the difficulties and open doors they present on a worldwide scale.

The Worldwide Fintech Blast

The fintech area has encountered dramatic development on a worldwide scale, changing how monetary administrations are conveyed, consumed, and managed. A few key elements have added to the worldwide fintech blast:

Innovation Headways: The fast improvement of advancements like portable registering, man-made reasoning, blockchain, and distributed computing has established a helpful climate for fintech development.

Purchaser Interest: Expanding buyer assumptions for comfort, straightforwardness, and customized monetary administrations have driven the reception of fintech arrangements.

Startup Biological systems: Flourishing fintech startup environments have arisen in major worldwide urban areas, drawing in speculation, ability, and pioneering soul.

Administrative Help: Numerous states and administrative bodies have upheld fintech development by presenting sandboxes, decreasing administrative obstructions, and advancing monetary consideration.

Financial backer Premium: Institutional and funding financial backers have shown areas of strength for a for fintech ventures, encouraging the development of fintech firms around the world.

The Worldwide Neobank Peculiarity

Neobanks, a subset of fintech organizations, have likewise extended fundamentally on a worldwide scale. They have separated themselves by giving advanced just financial administrations that challenge customary financial models. Key components of the worldwide neobank peculiarity include:

Branchless Activities: Neobanks work without actual branches, diminishing above expenses and offering practical and client driven monetary administrations.

Client Driven Approach: Neobanks focus on client experience, frequently offering easy to use versatile applications, straightforward charge structures, and responsive client assistance.

Innovation Driven Arrangements: Cutting edge innovation, including man-made brainpower, information investigation, and distributed computing, empowers neobanks to offer imaginative administrations and customized monetary arrangements.

Worldwide Reach: Numerous neobanks offer administrations that help cross-line exchanges, giving serious unfamiliar trade rates to clients with global monetary interests.

Monetary Consideration: Neobanks have gained ground in advancing monetary incorporation by offering streamlined onboarding processes and open record the board.

Provincial Contrasts in Fintech and Neobanking

The fintech and neobanking scenes shift across districts, formed by variables like administrative conditions, market development, and nearby customer inclinations. Here is a concise outline of how these areas are developing in various regions of the planet:

North America:

The US and Canada have flourishing fintech environments, with an emphasis on computerized installments, loaning, and insurtech.

Neobanks have picked up speed, and their development is driven by purchaser interest for simple to-utilize and practical financial administrations.

Europe:

European nations have embraced fintech, with a solid accentuation on administrative development.

Neobanks, including N26, Revolut, and Monzo, have acquired conspicuousness for their easy to understand interfaces and serious expense structures.

Asia-Pacific:

Asia is a worldwide fintech area of interest, with business sectors like China, India, and Singapore at the cutting edge.

Advanced wallets and versatile installments have seen amazing reception, while neobanks like WeBank in China are reshaping the financial scene.

Latin America:

Latin American nations are encountering huge fintech development, tending to the necessities of unbanked and underbanked populaces.

Neobanks, as Nubank in Brazil, are giving simple admittance to banking administrations through portable applications.

Africa:

Africa is arising as a fintech pioneer, especially in versatile monetary administrations and blockchain arrangements.

Portable cash stages, like M-Pesa, have empowered monetary consideration and computerized installments across the landmass.

Center East:

The Center East has seen a flood in fintech movement, especially in the Unified Middle Easterner Emirates and Saudi Arabia.

Islamic fintech, consistent with Sharia standards, has likewise gotten momentum in the

locale.

Worldwide Patterns in Fintech and Neobanking

A few key worldwide patterns are forming the fintech and neobanking scene:

Computerized Installments: The reception of advanced wallets, portable installments, and contactless exchanges keeps on rising all around the world. These techniques offer accommodation and speed.

Blockchain and Digital money: Premium in blockchain innovation and cryptographic forms of money, especially Bitcoin and Ethereum, is developing. They are viewed as potential disruptors in the monetary and venture areas.

Administrative Development: Controllers are adjusting to the fintech scene by presenting guidelines that offset advancement with shopper insurance and monetary security.

Supportability and ESG: Ecological, Social, and Administration (ESG) contemplations are turning out to be progressively significant, with fintech firms offering feasible money choices.

Organizations and Biological systems: Fintech organizations are framing key associations with conventional banks and other specialist co-ops to make incorporated monetary environments that offer many administrations.

Difficulties and Open doors

The worldwide scene of fintech and neobanking presents the two difficulties and open doors for different partners:

Administrative Difficulties: Complying to advancing worldwide guidelines can be mind boggling for fintech firms and neobanks. They should guarantee consistence while exploring an interwoven of provincial and public necessities.

Network safety Dangers: As advanced monetary administrations become more broad, the gamble of digital dangers and information breaks increments. Suppliers need to put resources into strong network safety measures to safeguard client information.

Rivalry and Solidification: The serious scene is strengthening, with additional players entering the fintech and neobanking areas. This might prompt union as bigger organizations obtain more modest ones to extend their market reach.

Monetary Incorporation: Fintech and neobanking offer the possibility to connect monetary consideration holes by giving financial administrations to unbanked and underbanked populaces. These administrations can engage people and organizations in underserved areas.

Worldwide Openness: Cross-line exchanges and cutthroat unfamiliar trade rates are making everything fair for people and organizations with global monetary interests.

Development and Client Centricity: The emphasis on advancement and client driven administrations provokes conventional banks to adjust and work on their contributions, prompting better monetary items and administrations for customers.

Chapter 9

The Future Of Banking

The fate of banking is being molded by a juncture of mechanical headways, moving client assumptions, and developing administrative scenes. Conventional financial models are going through critical changes as monetary organizations adjust to the computerized age. This article dives into the vital patterns and improvements that are characterizing the fate of banking and reshaping the manner in which we deal with our funds.

Advanced Change

One of the most conspicuous and overall patterns molding the eventual fate of banking is computerized change. Banks are changing from customary physical branches to advanced first foundations. This is the way this change is showing:

On the web and Versatile Banking: The expansion of on the web and portable financial administrations permits clients to lead a large number of monetary exercises from their gadgets. This incorporates really looking at balances, making installments, moving assets, and in any event, applying for advances.

Computerized Just Banks: Neobanks, or advanced just banks, are building up some momentum with their branchless, simply advanced activities. They are portrayed by easy to use interfaces, straightforward charge structures, and imaginative elements.

Simulated intelligence and Mechanization: Man-made consciousness (artificial intelligence) and computerization are smoothing out different financial cycles, from client care chatbots to misrepresentation discovery. Simulated intelligence driven individual budget the executives instruments are likewise assisting clients with pursuing more educated monetary choices.

Blockchain and Conveyed Record Innovation: The reception of blockchain and appropriated record innovation is prompting safer and straightforward exchanges. It can possibly alter installments, exchange money, and personality check.

Open Banking: Open financial drives are advancing information dividing between monetary organizations and outsider suppliers. This cultivates contest and supports the improvement of new monetary items and administrations.

Client Driven Banking

The eventual fate of banking is client driven, zeroing in on upgrading the general financial experience. A few patterns are driving this shift:

Personalization: Banks are utilizing information examination and artificial intelligence to offer profoundly customized monetary items and administrations. Clients can get custom-made item proposals and speculation counsel.

Monetary Health: Banks are progressively zeroing in on their clients' monetary prosperity. They give instruments to planning, saving, and effective money management, assisting clients with accomplishing their monetary objectives.

all day, every day Openness: The digitalization of banking administrations guarantees that clients can get to their records and look for help nonstop. This availability improves consumer loyalty.

Versatile Installments and Computerized Wallets: The utilization of portable installment applications and advanced wallets is working on exchanges, permitting clients to pay for labor and products with a straightforward tap or sweep.

Improved Safety efforts

As banking turns out to be progressively advanced, safety efforts are developing to safeguard clients' delicate data. The accompanying patterns feature the accentuation on security coming down the line for banking:

Biometrics: Biometric validation strategies, like unique mark and facial acknowledgment, are becoming norm for getting versatile banking applications and exchanges.

Two-Element and Multifaceted Validation: Two-factor verification (2FA) and multifaceted confirmation (MFA) add extra layers of safety to check the personality of clients.

Blockchain-Based Security: Blockchain innovation is being utilized to get exchanges, offering straightforwardness and permanence that can forestall extortion and information breaks.

Network safety Measures: Banks are putting resources into cutting edge online protection answers for shield client information from digital dangers. Constant checking and danger discovery are indispensable to their security methodologies.

Ascent of Neobanks

Neobanks, otherwise called computerized just banks or challenger banks, are at the very front representing things to come of banking. These imaginative foundations have upset conventional financial models in more than one way:

No Actual Branches: Neobanks work solely on the web and don't keep up with physical branches, permitting them to work with lower above costs.

Easy to understand Applications: Neobanks offer easy to use portable applications that give a consistent financial encounter, from account opening to everyday exchanges.

Straightforward Charge Designs: Neobanks are known for their straightforward expense structures, frequently offering no-charge accounts and cutthroat unfamiliar trade rates.

Worldwide Availability: Numerous neobanks support cross-line exchanges and deal worldwide record access, taking special care of people and organizations with worldwide monetary interests.

Speedy Onboarding: Neobanks focus on productive onboarding processes, empowering clients to open records in no time, frequently with a basic photograph of ID and a couple of taps on a versatile application.

Man-made reasoning and Robotization

The coordination of computerized reasoning and mechanization is changing financial activities in significant ways:

Chatbots and Remote helpers: artificial intelligence fueled chatbots and remote helpers give client service, answer questions, and guide clients through different financial cycles.

Credit Scoring and Chance Evaluation: computer based intelligence calculations are further developing credit scoring and hazard appraisal processes, going with loaning choices quicker and more precise.

Misrepresentation Recognition: artificial intelligence driven extortion identification frameworks can distinguish abnormalities and possible dangers, assisting keeps money with safeguarding client resources.

Prescient Examination: Banks utilize prescient investigation to expect client needs, empowering them to offer customized items and administrations.

Cryptographic money and Computerized Resources

Cryptographic forms of money and computerized resources are building up some forward momentum in the monetary business and are ready to assume a huge part in store for banking:

Computerized Monetary standards: National banks and legislatures are investigating the formation of computerized monetary forms, like the advanced yuan and advanced dollar, for of modernizing financial frameworks.

Decentralized Money (DeFi): DeFi stages are utilizing blockchain innovation to make decentralized monetary frameworks that proposition administrations like loaning, acquiring, and exchanging without customary middle people.

Institutional Reception: Institutional financial backers are progressively entering the cryptographic money space, showing developing standard acknowledgment.

Stablecoins: Stablecoins, which are digital forms of money fixed to true resources like the U.S. dollar, are becoming famous for their soundness and appropriateness for ordinary exchanges.

Feasible and Dependable Banking

The fate of banking is described by a developing accentuation on maintainability, morals, and social obligation:

Ecological, Social, and Administration (ESG) Financial planning: Banks are incorporating ESG rules into their speculation choices, giving clients chances to help supportable organizations and tasks.

Green Funding: Banks are advancing green supporting by offering credits and speculation items for harmless to the ecosystem drives.

Monetary Consideration: Banks are pursuing monetary incorporation, guaranteeing that underserved populaces approach fundamental financial administrations.

Difficulties and Contemplations

As the eventual fate of banking keeps on advancing, a few difficulties and contemplations come to the very front:

Administrative Consistence: Banks should explore a complex and developing administrative scene, guaranteeing they comply to monetary guidelines while seeking after creative arrangements.

Information Protection: Clients should believe that their own and monetary information is taken care of safely and secretly. Specialist organizations should comply with information insurance regulations and strategies.

Online protection Dangers: As computerized stages, banks are vulnerable to network safety dangers. They should put resources into hearty safety efforts to safeguard client information and exchanges.

Market Contest: The rising number of players in the monetary business is cultivating a profoundly cutthroat climate. Clients might have to research and contrast administrations with pick the ones that best address their issues.

Venture Dangers: While the eventual fate of banking offers assorted speculation open doors, clients should know about the dangers related with putting resources into monetary business sectors.

9.1Trends in Banking Technology

The financial business is going through a significant change driven by quick mechanical progressions, moving client assumptions, and developing administrative scenes. In this article, we will investigate the vital patterns in financial innovation, which are reshaping the manner in which monetary organizations work and collaborate with their clients.

Computerized Banking

The Ascent of On the web and Versatile Banking: Computerized banking, including on the web and portable administrations, has turned into a foundation of the cutting edge financial experience. Clients can now lead a great many monetary exercises, from really looking at balances to making installments, from the comfort of their gadgets.

Advanced Just Banks (Neobanks): Neobanks, otherwise called computerized just banks, are testing conventional financial models by working solely on the web. They offer straightforward charge structures, easy to use interfaces, and inventive highlights, making them an appealing choice for some clients.

Computerized Wallets and Portable Installments: The multiplication of advanced wallets and versatile installment applications has smoothed out exchanges. Clients can pay for labor and products with a basic tap or output, decreasing the requirement for actual money or cards.

The Effect of Coronavirus on Computerized Banking: The Coronavirus pandemic sped up the reception of advanced financial administrations. With social removing estimates set up, clients looked for contactless and remote financial choices, and large numbers of these progressions are probably going to continue in the post-pandemic world.

Man-made consciousness and Computerization

Artificial intelligence Controlled Chatbots and Menial helpers: Man-made consciousness (artificial intelligence) is reforming client care with the presentation of chatbots and remote helpers. These innovations give day in and day out help, noting questions and directing clients through different financial cycles.

Man-made intelligence in Hazard Appraisal and Credit Scoring: artificial intelligence is being utilized to improve risk evaluation and credit scoring processes. Overwhelmingly of information, computer based intelligence calculations can go with quicker and more precise loaning choices.

Prescient Examination and Personalization: Banks are utilizing prescient investigation to expect client needs. This empowers them to give profoundly customized item proposals and speculation exhortation, upgrading the general client experience.

Simulated intelligence in Misrepresentation Location and Avoidance: artificial intelligence driven extortion identification frameworks are turning out to be more complex. They can recognize inconsistencies and likely dangers with more prominent exactness, assisting saves money with safeguarding client resources.

Blockchain and Digital money

Figuring out Blockchain Innovation: Blockchain, at first produced for digital currencies, has tracked down applications a long ways past its underlying use. This innovation offers a solid and straightforward approach to recording and checking exchanges.

Digital forms of money in Banking: The ascent of cryptographic forms of money, especially Bitcoin and Ethereum, has disturbed customary financial frameworks. These computerized monetary forms are being coordinated into different monetary administrations and venture items.

Decentralized Money (DeFi): DeFi stages are utilizing blockchain innovation to make decentralized monetary frameworks. These stages offer administrations like loaning, acquiring, and exchanging without customary middle people.

National Bank Advanced Monetary forms (CBDCs): Numerous national banks are investigating the production of national bank computerized monetary forms (CB-DCs). These advanced portrayals of public monetary forms can possibly modernize money related frameworks.

Network protection in Banking

The Developing Significance of Network safety: With banking turning out to be progressively advanced, the significance of online protection has developed dramatically. Safeguarding client information and it is principal to keep up with trust.

Digital Dangers in Banking: Banks face a scope of digital dangers, including information breaks, phishing assaults, ransomware, and insider dangers. Understanding these dangers is fundamental for creating viable online protection procedures.

Techniques for Powerful Financial Online protection: This segment will frame methodologies and best practices for guaranteeing hearty network safety in the financial business. Points will incorporate danger discovery, occurrence reaction, and worker preparing.

Administrative Measures and Consistence: Administrative bodies overall are fixing their network safety prerequisites for monetary foundations. This part will analyze the administrative scene and examine the consistence challenges banks face.

Client Driven Banking

Personalization and Client Experience: The eventual fate of banking is client driven, with an emphasis on personalization and upgraded client encounters. Banks are utilizing information and innovation to offer exceptionally customized monetary items and administrations.

Monetary Wellbeing and Individual accounting The executives: Banks are advancing monetary health by giving instruments to planning, saving, and money management. Clients can accomplish their monetary objectives with the assistance of inventive monetary administration stages.

Open Banking and Information Sharing: Open financial drives are advancing information dividing between monetary establishments and outsider suppliers. This pattern empowers the improvement of new monetary items and administrations and permits clients to get to a more extensive scope of administrations.

Manageable and Moral Banking: Banks are progressively coordinating natural, social, and administration (ESG) contemplations into their tasks. Manageable and moral banking is turning into a fundamental part of the business.

The Fate of Banking

The Advancement of Conventional Banking: Customary financial models are developing quickly to adjust to the computerized age. This segment will investigate how banks are changing from actual branches to advanced first establishments.

The Job of Advanced Change: Computerized change is at the core representing things to come of banking. This segment will examine how innovation is reshaping customary financial cycles and making a more open and proficient monetary biological system.

Administrative Changes and Monetary Consideration: Administrative changes are working with monetary incorporation by diminishing obstructions and advancing the reception of creative monetary arrangements.

Worldwide Patterns and Local Contrasts: The eventual fate of banking isn't uniform across the globe. This segment will investigate territorial contrasts in financial innovation reception and feature key patterns in different districts.

Difficulties and Contemplations

Administrative Consistence: Complying to advancing worldwide guidelines is complicated for banks and monetary foundations. This part will talk about the difficulties and contemplations connected with administrative consistence.

Information Security and Morals: The treatment of individual and monetary information is foremost. This part will investigate the difficulties and moral contemplations encompassing information protection and security.

Network protection Dangers: As banks progressively depend on advanced stages, the gamble of network safety dangers poses a potential threat. This segment will cover the online protection challenges banks face and how they can relieve these dangers.

Market Rivalry and Client Mindfulness: The developing number of players in the banking and fintech areas is encouraging extreme contest. Clients should know about the choices accessible and pick benefits that line up with their necessities.

Speculation Dangers in Monetary Business sectors: The eventual fate of banking offers different venture valuable open doors, yet clients should know about the dangers related with putting resources into monetary business sectors. This part will investigate the venture scene in banking.

9.2The Role of Quantum Computing

Quantum registering is a quickly propelling field that holds the commitment of upsetting how we process and break down information. Dissimilar to traditional PCs, which depend on parallel pieces (0s and 1s), quantum PCs use quantum bits or qubits, which can exist in numerous states all the while because of the standards of superposition and snare. This article investigates the arising job of quantum processing in the advanced world and the potential it offers in different areas.

Improving Computational Power

Quantum PCs can possibly dramatically increment computational power for explicit assignments. While traditional PCs process information consecutively, quantum PCs can investigate various arrangements at the same time. This benefit can be especially significant in taking care of mind boggling advancement issues, which have applications in different fields, including money, operations, and cryptography.

For example, quantum figuring can significantly upgrade the effectiveness of monetary demonstrating and risk evaluation, empowering more precise expectations and informed speculation choices. In operations, it can enhance courses for delivery and transportation, decreasing expenses and natural effect.

Breaking Current Cryptography

One of the most broadly examined ramifications of quantum processing is its capacity to break current encryption strategies. Traditional PCs would call for an unfeasible measure of investment to break complex encryption keys, yet quantum PCs can play out the undertaking a lot quicker because of their capacity to proficiently factor enormous numbers dramatically more.

Therefore, current cryptographic methods, for example, RSA and ECC, which are broadly used to get online interchanges and exchanges, could become defenseless. To address this, specialists are effectively chipping away at post-quantum cryptography that can endure assaults from quantum PCs. The job of quantum figuring in the area of cryptography is a blade that cuts both ways, representing a security danger while likewise driving development in encryption techniques.

Drug Disclosure and Materials Science

Quantum figuring can altogether speed up drug revelation and materials science. Recreating sub-atomic communications at a quantum level is a profoundly complicated task that old style PCs battle with. Quantum PCs can play out these recreations with a lot more noteworthy proficiency.

Drug organizations can utilize quantum figuring to find new medications and break down their expected effect on the human body, in this manner facilitating the medication advancement process. In materials science, it can assist analysts with planning new materials with wanted properties, making the way for advancements in energy capacity, hardware, and that's just the beginning.

AI and Man-made reasoning

Quantum processing can assume a vital part in improving AI and man-made consciousness. Quantum AI calculations can process and investigate tremendous datasets with remarkable speed, prompting more exact expectations and more proficient preparation of simulated intelligence models.

For example, quantum PCs can be utilized to improve the preparation of brain organizations, which underlie numerous computer based intelligence applications. They can likewise be applied in fields like regular language handling, picture acknowledgment, and suggestion frameworks, where the capacity to rapidly deal with huge datasets is critical.

Monetary Displaying and Hazard Investigation

In the monetary business, quantum processing is ready to upset how we model complex monetary frameworks and survey risk. The capacity to deal with huge datasets and complex reenactments continuously can prompt more precise and opportune monetary expectations.

Venture companies can profit from quantum registering by streamlining exchanging techniques, portfolio the executives, and hazard evaluation. Furthermore, banks and monetary foundations can upgrade their network safety frameworks to safeguard against quantum figuring controlled assaults.

Environment Displaying and Natural Effect Appraisal

Environment displaying and natural effect evaluation are basic regions where quantum registering can have a significant impact. Anticipating the impacts of environmental change, recreating natural frameworks, and understanding complex barometrical collaborations are computationally escalated undertakings.

Quantum PCs can speed up these recreations, giving more precise and convenient information to address natural difficulties. This innovation can assist us with better comprehension environment patterns, evaluate the ecological effect of different exercises, and foster methodologies to moderate environmental change.

Enhancing Supply Chains and Strategies

Production network the board and strategies are mind boggling fields that include various factors and conditions. Quantum processing's capacity to take care of improvement issues can alter these areas by tracking down the most productive courses, limiting expenses, and lessening asset squander.

Organizations can utilize quantum processing to advance stock administration, course arranging, and conveyance, bringing about diminished carbon impressions and more manageable activities.

The Rush to Quantum Incomparability

Quantum incomparability, a term instituted by specialists, alludes forthright at which quantum PCs can perform errands past the range of old style PCs. Accomplishing quantum matchless quality is a critical achievement in the improvement of quantum figuring, as it exhibits the down to earth prevalence of quantum PCs in unambiguous applications.

Organizations like Google and IBM are effectively contending to accomplish quantum matchless quality, and this race has powered fast headways in the field. When quantum matchless quality is reached, the job of quantum figuring in different enterprises will turn out to be significantly more articulated.

9.3Financial Inclusion and Digital Banking

Monetary incorporation, the most common way of guaranteeing that people and networks approach reasonable and suitable monetary administrations, is a basic worldwide test. Computerized banking has arisen as an amazing asset in progressing monetary consideration by furnishing underserved populaces with admittance to fundamental monetary administrations. In this article, we will investigate the connection between monetary consideration and computerized banking, featuring the manners by which innovation is spanning the monetary separation and growing financial open doors for millions all over the planet.

Computerized Banking: A Door to Monetary Incorporation

Computerized banking, incorporating on the web and versatile financial administrations, offers a helpful and practical method for coming to underserved populaces.

The capacity to get to monetary administrations through cell phones and PCs has turned into a unique advantage in the drive for monetary consideration. This is the way computerized banking adds to this significant objective:

Availability: Advanced banking takes out topographical hindrances. People in remote or underserved regions can get to banking administrations without the requirement for an actual branch. This makes banking administrations more comprehensive and accessible to a more extensive populace.

Reasonableness: Conventional banking frequently includes high exchange expenses and least equilibrium necessities. Advanced financial arrangements are commonly more practical, with lower or no expenses, empowering people with restricted monetary assets to partake in the conventional financial framework.

Accommodation: Advanced financial proposals nonstop admittance to monetary administrations. Clients can check adjusts, move reserves, take care of bills, and more whenever it might suit them. This availability is especially worthwhile for those with occupied timetables or restricted portability.

Security: High level safety efforts in advanced financial applications safeguard client information and exchanges. This improved security imparts trust in clients, making them bound to draw in with computerized monetary administrations.

Conquering Hindrances to Monetary Incorporation

Monetary incorporation isn't just about giving admittance to ledgers; it's tied in with offering a scope of monetary items and administrations that take special care of the different necessities of people and organizations. Computerized banking is strategically set up to address a few vital obstructions to monetary incorporation:

Absence of Foundation: In numerous locales, conventional financial framework is deficient. Computerized financial depends on the current media communications organization, making it a practical answer for regions without bank offices.

ID Difficulties: For those without formal distinguishing proof records, getting to customary financial administrations can challenge. Computerized financial stages are investigating imaginative arrangements like biometric recognizable proof, permitting people to make accounts without true records.

Distance and Travel Limitations: In far off regions, going to a bank office can be tedious and expensive. Advanced financial offers the capacity to get to monetary administrations without the requirement for long excursions, which can be especially troublesome for individuals in provincial regions.

Monetary Proficiency: Understanding how to utilize monetary administrations is significant for monetary incorporation. Computerized financial stages frequently give instructive assets and easy to understand points of interaction to assist clients with turning out to be all the more monetarily proficient.

Versatile Cash and Computerized Wallets

Versatile cash administrations, like M-Pesa in Kenya, have been instrumental in progressing monetary consideration. These administrations permit people to store, pull out, and move cash through their cell phones, successfully transforming the telephone into a computerized wallet. Clients can likewise pay for labor and products, get government advantages, and even access credit and protection items.

Advanced wallets, for example, PayPal and Apple Pay, offer comparative advantages, making it simple for people to electronically store and move cash. These administrations have become fundamental in web based business and online exchanges, extending monetary access for the people who might not have conventional ledgers.

Microfinance and Distributed Loaning

Computerized banking has worked with the development of microfinance and distributed (P2P) loaning stages. These stages associate moneylenders and borrowers, frequently focusing on little and miniature organizations that might not approach conventional credits. By going through with these exchanges on the web, borrowers can get to capital all the more effectively, prompting financial strengthening and business development.

Computerized microfinance has been especially successful in arising economies, where little credits can considerably affect pioneering tries. Additionally, P2P loaning stages democratize the loaning system, permitting people to put resources into the progress of others and procure profits from their ventures.

Monetary Incorporation Drives and Guidelines

States and administrative specialists overall are perceiving the significance of monetary incorporation and computerized banking. They are executing arrangements and guidelines that energize the development of advanced banking while at the same time guaranteeing shopper assurance and information security.

For instance, a few legislatures expect banks to offer essential, no-charge records to the unbanked populace. Also, guidelines frequently command that computerized financial stages comply to severe security and information assurance norms, further upgrading trust among clients.

Difficulties and Contemplations

While computerized banking is an incredible asset for progressing monetary incorporation, it isn't without its difficulties and contemplations:

Computerized Gap: The advanced separation, which alludes to the hole between the people who approach computerized innovations and the individuals who don't, stays a huge test. Many individuals, especially in remote or devastated districts, actually need admittance to the web and cell phones.

Online protection Worries: With the development of computerized banking, network safety turns into an essential concern. Safeguarding client information and monetary exchanges is fundamental to keeping up with trust in advanced financial stages.

Security Issues: The assortment and utilization of client information by computerized financial suppliers raise significant protection concerns. Controllers and industry partners should figure out some kind of harmony among advancement and information insurance.

Monetary Proficiency: To completely saddle the advantages of advanced banking, people should be monetarily proficient. Training and mindfulness programs are important to guarantee that clients comprehend how to utilize computerized financial administrations really.

9.4Social and Environmental Responsibility

Social and natural obligation, frequently alluded to as corporate social obligation (CSR) or maintainability, is a basic system that urges associations to offset benefit having with their effect on society and the climate. In a period where issues like environmental change, social imbalance, and asset exhaustion request aggregate activity, the job of social and ecological obligation is a higher priority than any time in recent memory. This article investigates the importance, standards, difficulties, and advantages of social and natural obligation, stressing its part in molding a manageable future for our planet.

The Meaning of Social and Ecological Obligation

Tending to Natural Difficulties

As the worldwide populace develops and financial exercises extend, the stress on our planet's assets and biological systems has turned into a squeezing concern. Social and natural obligation gives a system to organizations to limit their ecological effect by diminishing discharges, monitoring assets, and carrying out manageable practices.

By adjusting their tasks to ecological objectives, organizations can add to relieving environmental change, protecting biodiversity, and shielding normal assets.

Advancing Social Uniformity and Incorporation

Social obligation envelops endeavors to make a fair and comprehensive society. By rehearsing social obligation, associations can assist with lessening disparity, work on working circumstances, and backing underestimated networks. This advantages society all in all as well as improve an organization's standing and representative fulfillment. Social obligation programs frequently center around regions like training, medical services, and destitution mitigation to address basic cultural difficulties.

Improving Corporate Standing and Brand Worth

Organizations that effectively take part in friendly and natural obligation are much of the time apparent all the more well by purchasers. An association that exhibits a guarantee to supportability and moral practices can fabricate areas of strength for a, draw in a reliable client base, and separate itself in a serious commercial center. The positive public picture made by capable practices can upgrade an organization's standing and add to its drawn out progress.

Standards of Social and Ecological Obligation

Straightforwardness and Responsibility

Straightforwardness is an essential guideline of social and natural obligation. Associations should convey straightforwardly about their manageability endeavors, including their objectives, activities, and progress. Responsibility remains closely connected with straightforwardness, guaranteeing that organizations get a sense of ownership with their activities and are considered responsible for their social and ecological effects.

Moral Administration

Moral administration is basic for adjusting an organization's dynamic cycles with capable practices. This incorporates the advancement of sets of principles and lead, adherence to fair work norms, and the reconciliation of moral contemplations into business procedures and tasks.

Partner Commitment

Drawing in with partners, including representatives, clients, networks, and investors, is fundamental for guaranteeing that an association's social and ecological endeavors are very much educated and successful.

Partner commitment takes into account the distinguishing proof of key worries and the advancement of techniques that answer those worries.

Natural Stewardship

Ecological stewardship includes the dependable administration and protection of normal assets. Organizations that are earth capable endeavor to limit their environmental impression by lessening waste, preserving energy, and embracing feasible practices all through their stock chains.

Social Commitment

Social obligation incorporates endeavors to resolve cultural issues and contribute decidedly to networks. This can envelop drives, for example, supporting neighborhood training programs, subsidizing medical care projects, and effectively taking part in misfortune aid ventures.

Difficulties of Social and Ecological Obligation

Adjusting Benefit and Obligation

One of the essential difficulties of social and ecological obligation is offsetting monetary benefit with moral and feasible practices. Organizations frequently face strain to expand momentary benefits, which can be in conflict with long haul maintainability objectives. Finding some kind of harmony is an intricate undertaking that requires cautious preparation and responsibility.

Estimating Effect and Progress

Estimating the social and natural effect of liability endeavors can challenge. It frequently includes evaluating complicated, long haul results, making it challenging to measure achievement. Organizations should foster successful estimation and announcing systems to precisely follow progress.

Administrative Consistence

Consenting to an always advancing scene of ecological and social guidelines presents a continuous test for associations. Keeping awake to-date with developing regulations and guaranteeing that strategic policies line up with these necessities can be asset serious.

Public Suspicion

A few people and gatherings still have a few doubts of corporate social obligation endeavors, associating them with being simple promoting strategies. Organizations should be veritable and straightforward in their obligation to obligation to conquer this distrust and fabricate trust.

Inventory network Intricacy

Obligation endeavors stretch out to supply chains, which can be complicated and include various accomplices. Guaranteeing that all providers stick to moral and economical practices can be a huge test, requiring cautious observing and coordinated effort.

Advantages of Social and Natural Obligation

Improved Standing and Brand Unwaveringness

Organizations that focus on friendly and natural obligation frequently partake in a more sure open picture. This prompts upgraded brand devotion, a bigger client base, and expanded seriousness in the commercial center.

Further developed Worker Fulfillment and Maintenance

Showing a pledge to social and ecological obligation can draw in and hold top ability. Representatives are many times more fulfilled working for organizations that line up with their own qualities and moral norms.

Risk Relief

Social and natural obligation endeavors can help organizations recognize and moderate dangers. By resolving issues proactively, associations lessen the probability of reputational harm, lawful difficulties, and administrative fines.

Development and Effectiveness

Mindful practices frequently drive development. Organizations that put resources into economical innovations and cycles find new efficiencies that can prompt expense reserve funds and upper hands.

Admittance to New Business sectors

Social and ecological obligation can open ways to new business sectors and open doors. Organizations that meet explicit manageability models might get to business sectors with an inclination for earth and socially dependable items and administrations.

Long haul Practicality

Feasible practices add to the drawn out feasibility of organizations. By decreasing ecological effects and upgrading social commitments, organizations guarantee their activities are viable with advancing worldwide difficulties.

Chapter10

Challenges And Ethical Considerations

In the complicated embroidery of contemporary society, we face various difficulties and moral contemplations that shape our activities and choices. From the determined development of innovation to the major problems of civil rights and natural manageability, our reality is set apart by a nonstop transaction of moral situations and reasonable issues. In this article, we will investigate a horde of difficulties and moral contemplations that defy us in the cutting edge age, featuring the intricacies they present and the significance of moral appearance in tending to them.

The Moral Contemplations of Innovative Progression

Security in the Advanced Age

As innovation progressively pervades each part of our lives, the assortment and utilization of individual information raise huge moral worries. With the multiplication of observation, information breaks, and the adaptation of individual data, people are defied with an essential moral inquiry: How might we safeguard our security in the computerized age? Moral contemplations encompassing information security request strong regulation, reliable corporate practices, and individual consciousness of the results of sharing individual data.

Man-made brainpower and Computerization

The ascent of man-made brainpower (computer based intelligence) and mechanization presents moral problems, particularly with regards to business. As simulated intelligence frameworks and robots become more skilled, there is the potential for broad work removal. Moral contemplations rotate around guaranteeing a simply progress for laborers, advancing reskilling and upskilling, and tending to the financial and social outcomes of robotization.

Algorithmic Predisposition and Reasonableness

Calculations assume an undeniably conspicuous part in dynamic cycles, from employing to law enforcement. Moral worries arise when calculations display inclinations in light of race, orientation, or different elements, prompting uncalled for results.

Tending to algorithmic predisposition requires straightforwardness, responsibility, and a guarantee to decency.

Civil rights and Fairness

Racial and Social Imbalance

The tireless racial and social imbalances that penetrate contemporary society stay a grave test. Moral contemplations request that we defy foundational prejudice, address abberations in training, medical services, and law enforcement, and work toward genuine equity and civil rights.

Orientation Value and Inclusivity

Orientation uniformity and inclusivity are essential moral objectives. Handling issues, for example, the orientation pay hole, underrepresentation of ladies in positions of authority, and separation in view of orientation character are key parts of contemporary civil rights.

LGBTQ+ Freedoms

The LGBTQ+ people group faces progressing separation and disparities. Moral contemplations highlight the significance of legitimate assurances, acknowledgment, and equivalent freedoms for all people, paying little mind to sexual direction or orientation personality.

Natural Obligation and Maintainability

Environmental Change

Environmental change is a squeezing worldwide test with significant moral ramifications. As the results of environmental change, for example, outrageous climate occasions and rising ocean levels, lopsidedly influence weak networks, moral contemplations request quick and broad activity. The moral problem is whether we have an honest conviction to safeguard the climate for people in the future.

Biodiversity and Biological system Safeguarding

The speeding up loss of biodiversity and biological systems undermines the fragile equilibrium of our planet. Moral contemplations include protecting the world's environments, recognizing our interconnectedness with nature, and rehearsing mindful stewardship.

Asset Consumption and Natural Equity

Asset consumption, including issues like water shortage and deforestation, brings up moral issues about who endures the worst part of these natural difficulties. Addressing asset consumption morally requires a promise to impartial asset dissemination and limiting mischief to underestimated networks.

Medical care and Clinical Morals

Admittance to Medical care

Admittance to quality medical care stays a worldwide moral concern. The test is to guarantee medical care is reasonable and open to all, regardless of financial status, tending to wellbeing incongruities and moral inquiries concerning value and human pride.

Moral Quandaries in Clinical Advances

Propels in medication, like quality altering and organ transplantation, present moral difficulties. Questions emerge about the restrictions of logical intercession, moral therapy of examination subjects, and the fair appropriation of health advantages.

End-of-Life Care and Willful extermination

Moral contemplations in medical services stretch out to end-of-life care and killing. The mind boggling and delicate nature of these issues calls for vigorous moral structures that regard individual independence while guaranteeing the best expectations of clinical morals.

Worldwide Difficulties and Moral Obligations

Compassionate Emergencies and Evacuees

Compassionate emergencies, frequently determined by struggle and natural fiascos, challenge us to wrestle with moral obligations. Inviting exiles, giving guide to those out of luck, and pushing for harmony are vital moral contemplations.

Worldwide Financial Imbalance

The obvious variations in worldwide riches and financial imbalance are principal moral issues. Inquiries of fair exchange, worldwide monetary frameworks, and global collaboration are basic for tending to these difficulties.

Moral Utilization of Force and Impact

Moral contemplations reach out to the mindful activity of force and impact. In governmental issues, business, and different spaces, moral administration requires a pledge to equity, responsibility, and moral direction.

10.1Data Privacy and Ethics

In an undeniably digitized world, information protection and morals have become crucial contemplations. As private data is gathered, handled, and shared at an extraordinary scale, concerns encompassing information security, moral information use, and the harmony between mechanical progression and individual freedoms have come to the front. This article investigates the crossing point of information security and morals, tending to the difficulties, standards, and outcomes of our computerized age.

Challenges in Information Security and Morals

Information Assortment and Reconnaissance

With the expansion of savvy gadgets, applications, and online stages, our lives have become progressively interconnected with the computerized domain. This interconnectedness has prompted broad information assortment, frequently without people's express assent. The test lies in the moral ramifications of unavoidable observation and the potential for misuse.

Information Breaks and Network safety

Information breaks, where unapproved parties get sufficiently close to delicate data, have turned into really quite normal. These breaks can have extreme ramifications for people and associations. Moral contemplations rotate around the dependable treatment of information, network safety measures, and the straightforwardness of organizations when breaks happen.

Client Assent and Straightforwardness

Numerous advanced administrations depend on client assent for information assortment. In any case, the complicated language and assent shapes frequently introduced to clients can be confounding or deluding. Guaranteeing educated and deliberate assent, as well as straightforwardness in information rehearses, is a huge moral test.

Information Profiling and Segregation

The utilization of calculations to profile people and simply decide, like in recruiting, loaning, or promoting, can bring about out of line or biased results. Moral contemplations underline the significance of decency, responsibility, and non-segregation in mechanized dynamic cycles.

Standards of Information Protection and Morals

Straightforwardness and Informed Assent

Straightforwardness is a basic rule of information security and morals. People ought to be educated about the information gathered, how it will be utilized, and the gatherings in question. Assent ought to be openly given, informed, and revocable, guaranteeing people have command over their information.

Information Minimization

Associations ought to just gather information that is fundamental for the planned reason. The standard of information minimization underlines that organizations ought to keep away from superfluous or unreasonable information assortment.

Information Security and Assurance

Defending information against breaks and unapproved access is a moral goal. Associations should put resources into powerful network safety measures to safeguard delicate data.

Fair and Non-Unfair Utilization of Information

Information ought not be utilized in manners that oppress people or gatherings in light of elements like race, orientation, or financial status. Moral information use guarantees decency and inclusivity in dynamic cycles.

Responsibility and Obligation

Associations and people are responsible for their activities in taking care of information. Responsibility involves assuming a sense of ownership with information insurance and moral information rehearses, which might include consistence with information security guidelines.

Information Anonymization and De-ID

Anonymization and de-ID procedures safeguard protection by guaranteeing that information can't be followed back to a person. These strategies maintain the moral guideline of safeguarding individual characters.

Results of Moral Information Use

Improved Trust and Notoriety

Moral information use cultivates trust among associations and their clients or clients. At the point when people feel that their information is dealt with dependably and morally, it reinforces the standing of the association.

Consistence with Guidelines

Moral information rehearses line up with information security guidelines, like the Overall Information Assurance Guideline (GDPR) in Europe or the California Shopper Protection Act (CCPA) in the US. Consistence with these guidelines is both a moral and legitimate liability.

Risk Relief

Moral information rehearses assist with relieving the dangers related with information breaks and possible legitimate repercussions. By focusing on information assurance and moral use, associations diminish the probability of unfavorable occasions.

Development and Business Achievement

Moral information use advances dependable development. It empowers associations to saddle the force of information while regarding individual freedoms and cultural standards, adding to business achievement and cultural advantages.

Moral Quandaries in Arising Advances

Man-made brainpower and AI

As artificial intelligence and AI frameworks go with independent choices in light of information, moral situations emerge. Inquiries concerning responsibility for man-made intelligence choices, the potential for algorithmic predisposition, and the ramifications for work are integral to this arising field.

Biometric Information and Facial Acknowledgment

The utilization of biometric information, like facial acknowledgment, raises huge moral worries. Issues incorporate assent for facial acknowledgment, its utilization in observation, and the potential for abuse.

IoT and Shrewd Gadgets

The Web of Things (IoT) interfaces regular gadgets to the web, empowering information assortment and interconnectivity. Moral difficulties remember guaranteeing information security for IoT gadgets and tending to the protection ramifications of broad information assortment.

Adjusting Innovative Headway and Information Morals

Offsetting mechanical headway with information morals is a basic test in the computerized age. The quick advancement of innovation has dominated the improvement of moral systems and guidelines.

Finding some kind of harmony requires continuous discourse and joint effort among partners, including government, industry, and common society. It likewise requires a guarantee to moral contemplations in exploration, improvement, and execution of arising advances.

10.2The Digital Divide

The computerized partition is a multi-layered issue that portrays the variations in admittance to and utilization of computerized advances among people, networks, and nations. In the present profoundly interconnected world, admittance to the web and computerized devices has become key to support in training, the work market, medical services, and metro commitment. This article dives into the intricacies of the computerized partition, its suggestions, and the endeavors being made to overcome this issue and make a more comprehensive computerized society.

Grasping the Advanced Gap

The computerized partition is certainly not a particular issue yet rather an intricate arrangement of inconsistencies that incorporate a few aspects:

Access Separation: This aspect alludes to the disparity in admittance to web framework and computerized gadgets. Numerous people group, especially in rustic or financially burdened regions, need admittance to dependable internet providers or present day gadgets, putting them in a difficult situation.

Use Gap: In any event, when access is free, variations exist in how people and networks utilize advanced advancements. Some might miss the mark on computerized proficiency abilities expected to use innovation really, thwarting their capacity to get to instructive assets, open positions, and fundamental administrations.

Quality Gap: Abberations in the nature of web associations and gadgets additionally add to the advanced gap. Fast web is in many cases fundamental for exercises like remote work or web based learning, and those with lower-quality associations might be prohibited from these open doors.

Reasonableness Separation: The expense of computerized gadgets and internet providers can be a huge boundary for some people and families, especially those with restricted monetary means. The reasonableness partition frequently converges with different elements of the computerized partition.

Ramifications of the Advanced Separation

The advanced separation has expansive ramifications that touch on different parts of present day life:

Instruction: The Coronavirus pandemic featured the computerized gap's effect on training. Understudies without admittance to web based learning assets confronted huge weaknesses in their scholarly advancement. This present circumstance featured the criticalness of connecting the advanced gap in schooling.

Work: Many open positions are presently just available on the web. Those without computerized abilities and admittance to the web are frequently barred from remote work choices, restricting their business possibilities.

Medical care: Telehealth administrations have become imperative for giving medical care, particularly in the midst of emergency. People without web access might confront obstructions to getting clinical exhortation and care.

Municipal Cooperation: The computerized separation can influence city commitment, as online stages and data dispersal progressively assume a part in political talk and support.

Financial Variations: The computerized separation can propagate and worsen existing monetary abberations, as people and networks without admittance to advanced assets battle to contend in an undeniably computerized economy.

Endeavors to Extension the Advanced Separation

Framework Development: States and confidential associations are putting resources into extending broadband foundation to reach underserved regions. Drives like the Government Interchanges Commission's (FCC) Rustic Advanced Open door Asset plan to carry high velocity web to provincial networks.

Advanced Incorporation Projects: Numerous associations and networks have sent off computerized consideration projects to give preparing and admittance to advanced assets. These projects offer computerized proficiency preparing and reasonable gadgets to underserved populaces.

Sponsorships and Help Projects: To address the reasonableness aspect of the advanced separation, state run administrations and associations offer endowments and help programs that assist low-pay people with getting to computerized innovations. For instance, the Life saver program in the US gives limits on telephone and internet providers for qualified low-pay families.

Public-Private Associations: Coordinated efforts between government offices and privately owned businesses can assist with stretching out web admittance to far off regions and give reasonable web access choices.

Gadget Dispersion: A few drives center around circulating computerized gadgets, similar to PCs or tablets, to understudies and underserved networks. These gadgets are fundamental for people to take part in web-based schooling and occupation looking for exercises.

Challenges in Spanning the Gap

Spanning the computerized partition is a perplexing and progressing challenge. A few variables add to the industriousness of this hole:

Cost and Financing: Growing framework, giving computerized proficiency preparing, and sponsoring web access all require significant subsidizing. Satisfactory monetary assets are expected to carry out viable arrangements.

Openness: Actual hindrances, similar to the geology of country regions, can confuse endeavors to grow admittance to computerized advancements.

Advanced Education: Computerized incorporation endeavors should address access as well as the improvement of computerized proficiency abilities. Guaranteeing that people can utilize advanced apparatuses successfully is significant to shutting the separation.

Manageability: Projects pointed toward spanning the computerized partition should be supportable over the long haul. Keeping up with and overhauling framework and proceeding with advanced consideration endeavors require progressing responsibility and assets.

Advanced Wellbeing and Security: As people get sufficiently close to computerized innovations, they likewise need instruction on computerized security and protection to safeguard themselves on the web.

10.3Security Risks and Mitigations

In a time characterized by advanced change and the interconnected idea of current culture, the significance of network safety couldn't possibly be more significant. The advanced scene is overflowing with security takes a chance with that can possibly upset organizations, compromise individual information, and undermine public safety. This article dives into the domain of network safety, investigating normal security gambles and the techniques and measures used to moderate them, guaranteeing the uprightness, classification, and accessibility of advanced resources.

Normal Security Dangers

Malware and Infections: Malevolent programming, or malware, envelops a great many dangers, including infections, worms, Trojans, and ransomware. These projects invade frameworks, bad or take information, and some of the time request a payoff for decoding keys.

Phishing Assaults: Phishing assaults include fooling people into uncovering individual or delicate data through underhanded messages, sites, or messages that have all the earmarks of being from dependable sources.

Information Breaks: Information breaks happen when delicate data is uncovered, frequently because of lacking safety efforts, frail passwords, or human blunder. These breaks can bring about the robbery of individual information, monetary misfortune, or reputational harm.

Conveyed Forswearing of Administration (DDoS) Assaults: DDoS assaults flood an organization or site with traffic, overpowering it and causing a help blackout. These assaults are frequently used to upset benefits or blackmail associations.

Insider Dangers: Insider dangers come from people inside an association, including representatives, workers for hire, or accomplices, who abuse their admittance to take information, commit misrepresentation, or harm frameworks.

Zero-Day Weaknesses: Zero-day weaknesses are blemishes in programming or equipment that are not yet known to the seller or people in general. Cybercriminals exploit these weaknesses before they can be fixed, hurting potential.

Inventory network Assaults: Cybercriminals compromise a provider's frameworks, programming, or equipment to penetrate an objective association through a confided in channel, taking advantage of the trust connection between the two.

Relief Methodologies and Measures

Antivirus and Hostile to Malware Programming: Executing vigorous antivirus and against malware arrangements can help distinguish and eliminate vindictive programming from frameworks. Standard updates are vital for stay safeguarded against advancing dangers.

Firewalls: Firewalls go about as a boundary between a confided in inward organization and outer organizations, separating and observing approaching and active traffic to impede pernicious exercises.

Email Sifting: Utilizing email separating arrangements can help distinguish and hinder phishing messages and malevolent connections before they arrive at beneficiaries' inboxes.

Encryption: Scrambling information both on the way and very still can defend it from unapproved access, regardless of whether a break happens. Solid encryption is central to safeguarding delicate data.

Access Control and Verification: Carrying out access controls areas of strength for and measures, for example, multifaceted confirmation (MFA), can restrict admittance to approved clients and gadgets.

Episode Reaction Plans: Creating and testing occurrence reaction plans empowers associations to respond rapidly and actually to security breaks, limiting likely harm.

Security Preparing and Mindfulness: Teaching workers about security chances, best practices, and how to perceive potential dangers like phishing assaults is fundamental in moderating insider dangers and raising the general security act.

Normal Fixing and Updates: Quickly applying programming and equipment updates and fixes helps address weaknesses and decrease the gamble of double-dealing.

Network Division: Dividing networks disengages delicate frameworks from less secure regions, restricting the sidelong development of aggressors inside the organization.

Outsider Gamble The executives: Associations ought to direct expected level of effort on outsider providers, including their security rehearses, to moderate the gamble of production network assaults.

Security Data and Occasion The executives (SIEM): SIEM frameworks gather and dissect security occasion information, giving bits of knowledge into potential security dangers and weaknesses.

Security Reviews and Entrance Testing: Normal security reviews and entrance testing can assist with recognizing shortcomings in an association's security pose, empowering proactive remediation.

Endpoint Security: Endpoint security arrangements safeguard individual gadgets, like workstations and cell phones, from malware and unapproved access.

Challenges in Alleviating Security Dangers

Advancing Danger Scene: Digital dangers are consistently advancing, with aggressors growing new strategies and procedures. Remaining in front of these arising dangers is really difficult for network safety experts.

Client Mindfulness and Instruction: Notwithstanding security preparing endeavors, human mistake stays a huge test. Clients might in any case succumb to phishing assaults or accidentally uncover delicate information.

Asset Imperatives: More modest associations, specifically, may miss the mark on assets and skill to execute extensive network safety measures, leaving them defenseless against assaults.

Adjusting Security and Convenience: Finding some kind of harmony between rigid safety efforts and ease of use can challenge. Excessively perplexing security techniques might deter clients from sticking to best practices.

Consistence and Guidelines: Consenting to online protection guidelines and industry norms can be a mind boggling task, requiring devoted assets and continuous carefulness.

Insider Dangers: Relieving insider dangers is testing since people with approved admittance might take advantage of their situations without raising doubt.

Arising Advances and Their Effect on Security

Man-made consciousness (artificial intelligence) and AI: simulated intelligence and AI are progressively utilized in network protection to recognize and answer dangers all the more quickly and precisely. Nonetheless, these advances can likewise be taken advantage of by aggressors to make more complex assaults.

IoT Security: The expansion of Web of Things (IoT) gadgets presents new security challenges. Guaranteeing the security of a wide exhibit of associated gadgets is essential in relieving possible weaknesses.

Blockchain Innovation: Blockchain innovation, known for its security highlights, is being investigated for use in different areas to safeguard information and upgrade trust.

10.4Balancing Innovation and Risk

Advancement and hazard are innately connected. While advancement fills progress, drives financial development, and upgrades our personal satisfaction, it likewise presents dangers and vulnerabilities. Finding some kind of harmony between cultivating advancement and overseeing chances is fundamental for long haul supportability and flourishing. This article investigates the powerful connection among development and hazard, the difficulties it postures, and techniques to actually explore this fragile balance.

The Powerful Connection Among Development and Hazard

Advancement is the driving force of progress, starting inventiveness, prodding monetary turn of events, and tending to cultural difficulties. From mechanical progressions and logical revelations to enterprising undertakings, development pushes us forward. Notwithstanding, every development conveys a component of hazard, both known and unexpected. These dangers can incorporate monetary, wellbeing, legitimate, reputational, and moral ramifications.

Challenges in Adjusting Development and Hazard

Feeling of dread toward Disappointment: The apprehension about disappointment can smother development. People and associations might be hesitant to face challenges, even determined ones, because of worries about pessimistic results. This hazard avoidance can upset the quest for novel thoughts and valuable open doors.

Asset Distribution: Adjusting the assignment of assets among advancement and gamble with the board can challenge. Overinvesting in development while ignoring risk the executives might prompt unanticipated weaknesses.

Momentary versus Long haul Gains: Advancement frequently implies momentary dangers for the commitment of long haul rewards. Finding some kind of harmony between prompt increases and the potential for more noteworthy future advantages is urgent.

Administrative Consistence: Fast advancement can once in a while dominate administrative structures. Associations need to explore the mind boggling landscape of consistence while keeping up with development energy.

Moral Predicaments: A few developments, especially in arising innovations, raise moral worries. Offsetting development with moral contemplations is indispensable to guarantee that progress lines up with cultural qualities and standards.

Methodologies for Adjusting Advancement and Hazard

Risk Appraisal and The executives: A thorough gamble appraisal process is fundamental for distinguishing, assessing, and moderating potential dangers related with development. It empowers associations to settle on informed conclusions about seeking after inventive undertakings.

Development Culture: Encouraging an advancement culture that values trial and error and gaining from disappointment is vital. Empowering workers to proceed with reasonable courses of action and giving a place of refuge to investigate novel thoughts can prompt advancement developments.

Light-footed and Versatile Methodology: Embracing a dexterous and versatile way to deal with advancement permits associations to answer gambles and changing conditions quickly. Persistent assessment and change are vital to overseeing developing dangers.

Administrative Commitment: Drawing in with administrative bodies right off the bat in the advancement cycle can assist adjust development to administrative consistence. Cooperative endeavors can likewise prompt more educated and adaptable administrative systems.

Moral Systems: Creating and complying to moral structures and rules is fundamental in exploring moral difficulties. Guaranteeing that development regards fundamental beliefs and moral standards encourages trust and acknowledgment.

Enhancement: Expanding development endeavors can assist with overseeing risk. Associations can put resources into an arrangement of inventive undertakings, spreading the gamble across different undertakings, as opposed to depending on a solitary, high-stakes development.

Certifiable Models

Space Investigation: The space business is a perfect representation of adjusting development and hazard. Space organizations and privately owned businesses push the limits of human information through imaginative advancements while overseeing gambles related with human spaceflight, specialized disappointments, and monetary ventures.

Drug Exploration: The drug business adjusts advancement and hazard in drug revelation and improvement. Making weighty drugs includes significant monetary speculations and clinical preliminary dangers, however the potential advantages are extraordinary.

Fintech: The monetary innovation area embraces advancement to alter banking and monetary administrations. Nonetheless, it additionally faces administrative, security, and moral difficulties, requiring cautious gamble the executives.